BRIGHT NOTES

THE MALTESE FALCON BY DASHIELL HAMMETT

Intelligent Education

Nashville, Tennessee

BRIGHT NOTES: The Maltese Falcon
www.BrightNotes.com

No part of this publication may be used or reproduced in any manner whatsoever without written permission, except in the case of brief quotations in critical articles and reviews. For permissions, contact Influence Publishers http://www.influencepublishers.com.

ISBN: 978-1-645420-76-7 (Paperback)
ISBN: 978-1-645420-77-4 (eBook)

Published in accordance with the U.S. Copyright Office Orphan Works and Mass Digitization report of the register of copyrights, June 2015.

Originally published by Monarch Press.
Walter James Miller
2020 Edition published by Influence Publishers.

Interior design by Lapiz Digital Services. Cover Design by Thinkpen Designs.

Printed in the United States of America.

Library of Congress Cataloging-in-Publication Data forthcoming.
Names: Intelligent Education
Title: BRIGHT NOTES: The Maltese Falcon
Subject: STU004000 STUDY AIDS / Book Notes

CONTENTS

1)	Introduction to Dashiell Hammett	1
2)	Textual Analysis	12
	Chapters 1 and 2	12
	Chapters 3 - 6	29
	Chapters 7 - 10	45
	Chapters 11 - 15	63
	Chapters 16 - 19	80
	Chapter 20	101
3)	Character Analyses	109
4)	Themes	129
5)	Plot Structure, Techniques, and Style	137
6)	Ideas for Papers, Oral Reports, and Class Discussion	154
7)	Bibliography	158

INTRODUCTION TO DASHIELL HAMMETT

LIFE, WORKS, AND REPUTATION OF DASHIELL HAMMETT (1894 - 1961)

The 1930 spring list of publisher Alfred A. Knopf included an action-detective novel. *The Maltese Falcon*, written by ex - "private eye" Dashiell Hammett. The year before, Knopf had published Hammett's first two novels, *Red Harvest* and *The Dain Curse*, and both were enjoying moderate success. Indeed, since 1923 Hammett had been known as one of the best detective-story writers in America. But now *The Maltese Falcon* launched him on two decades of fame and wealth as a "serious" (art) novelist whose characters became legendary figures in movie, radio, and TV drama as well as in printed literature.

Then, in the Fifties, broadcasters cut all ties with him, publishers let his books go out of print, his royalties were seized by the Federal government, and he was imprisoned for his leftist activities. Leaving jail mortally ill with lung trouble (exacerbated by his voluntary military service in World Wars I and II), he spent his final decade in near poverty, barely able to breathe. Somewhat enheartened by a strong renascence of his popularity in the late Fifties, he died in 1961. Today his reputation stands secure as one of the three major writers - the others are Mark Twain and Ernest Hemingway - who have done most to establish a genuine American prose style.

EARLY YEARS

Samuel Dashiell Hammett was born on May 27, 1894, on a failing farm in St. Mary's County, Maryland. Dashiell's father, Richard Hammett, was a heavy drinker, gambler, and womanizer, who held several successive jobs a year, and moved his family (Dashiell had a brother and sister), to Philadelphia and then to Baltimore. There Dashiell began his lifetime habit of reading voluminously, and this was probably a factor in his admission in 1908, to the prestigious Baltimore Polytechnic Institute. But just before his sixteenth birthday he had to drop out and go to work because his father's health failed. Dashiell held a series of jobs he hated: messenger, day laborer, machine operator. Finally, in 1915 he was rescued by an ad he read offering a job as "an operative" with the Pinkerton National Detective Agency.

HAMMETT AS "OP"

The Pinkerton Agency was founded by organizing genius Alan Pinkerton in 1850. Pinkerton's "ops" spied on the Confederates during the Civil War and solved many railroad robberies. By the time Hammett became an op, the Agency was specializing also in strike-breaking and union busting, and it was during these years that Hammett became aware of what he would later call "the class struggle." A second important influence during those years was the doctrine of James Wright, the Pinkerton administrator who trained Hammett. Wright was that kind of moralist who believes it's moral to use immoral methods against the immoral. An op could lie, cheat, blackmail, perjure himself, falsify the evidence, or intimidate and manipulate people, so long as he did it all to punish the suspect. In all these noble pursuits he must remain objective-he must neither hate nor love criminal nor client lest emotions interfere with his judgment and his ability to act decisively. This became part of the "code" of Hammett's private detectives, including Sam Spade, the protagonist of *The Maltese Falcon*.

[N.B. It was the Pinkerton private-detective agency's stationery that gave birth to the phrase "private eye." Their letterhead featured an all-seeing eye.]

WORLD WAR I SERVICE

Hammett interrupted his years of "tailing" missing persons and errant wives to enlist in the World War I U.S. Army. He became a sergeant in the Motor Ambulance Corps, and in administering to soldiers returning home during the catastrophic influenza epidemic of 1918, he caught the flu, and, his resistance weakened, became tubercular. Down to 140 pounds from his Pinkerton 160, he was awarded a $50.00 per month pension and discharged. After a period of convalescence, he went West and worked as a Pinkerton agent in Washington, Montana, and California.

MARRIAGE

Back in hospitals as a "lunger," he spent his weekend passes with a nurse named Jose Nolan. They married, settled down in San Francisco, and had two girls. Hammett, when well, worked part-time for Pinkerton: Jose described two days when he sat home in a daze after a "suspect he was tailing" led him into an alley and beat him with a brick. Confined to bed with TB about 20 hours a day, he decided to become a free-lance advertising writer. He had the good luck to be hired by Albert Samuels whose jewelry stores needed a copywriter and who became a kind of surrogate father for Dashiell. He bought an Underwood portable and began selling not only ad copy, but also short pieces to H. L. Mencken's "aristocrat among magazines," Smart Set, which paid him one cent a word. It was a natural next step for him to submit to the other Mencken "mag," *Black Mask*.

THE "CONTINENTAL OP"

Black Mask published detective and crime fiction by such stars as Erle Stanley Gardner and Carroll John Daly. Hammett saw in the new "hardboiled" fiction by Daly something he could improve upon: Hammett's great advantage was that he was one writer who had lived detective work; he had scars from head to shins inflicted by criminals. On October 1, 1923, *Black Mask* published Hammett's first "Continental Op" story: Pinkerton's National had become the Continental Agency, and James Wright, enhanced by Hammett, became the anonymous "Op." Soon *Black Mask* was giving Hammett top-billing with Gardner and Daly. The Op tells of his own experiences, in the first person ("I"), in twenty-six stories and novellas. We shall have occasion to look back on some of these early works in our "Textual Analysis" of *The Maltese Falcon*.

RED HARVEST

From November 1927 to February 1928 *Black Mask* ran four installments of a Hammett story that he then prepared for publication as a novel in book form. *Red Harvest* is based on his experience as a Pinkerton agent in mining towns. The mine owners have imported large numbers of Pinkerton gunmen to bust the Unions. But when the mercenary gunmen have destroyed the unions, they take over the town itself. When the Op arrives he proceeds to use the same technique that Sam Spade will use in Falcon-he plays one gangster against another until he has cleaned up the town. There is another important precedent in *Red Harvest*: His bloody work has dehumanized the Op. This, as William Marling has pointed out, "is environmental determinism: the hero understandably loses his morality in a murderous millieu."

THE DAIN CURSE

From November 1928 to February 1929, *Black Mask* serialized the early version of the novel *The Dain Curse* which Hammett also revised for publication by Knopf. It is the first novelized treatment in our literature of the religious cults in California. One of its distinctions is a running debate between Fitzstephan, a novelist, and the Op about what is real, what is fiction. This too helps pave the way for our "Textual Analysis" of Falcon. *The Dain Curse* was and still is criticized for its complex plot in which ten people are killed, two by the Op himself. One consequence of this adverse criticism is that Hammett decided that in *The Maltese Falcon* he would reduce the amount of bloodshed and have the four killings occur offstage.

MOVE TO NEW YORK

Late in 1929 Hammett borrowed $500 from Samuels and sent Jose and the girls to live in Los Angeles - where he hoped someday to get movie work - and he went to live in New York. When he ran out of funds, the young writer Nathanael West, night manager of a hotel, let Hammett register under a pseudonym (so he could not be traced if he had to leave without paying). There "Mr. T. Victrola Blueberry" worked on Falcon, read proofs for a West novel, and spent many a carousing night with West's friend William Faulkner.

THE MALTESE FALCON

From September 1929 to January 1930, *Black Mask* ran monthly installments of the story that Hammett then revised for publication in book form as *The Maltese Falcon*. The main character, Sam Spade, is a tougher, grimmer, more "on-the-run" private eye than the Continental Op would ever want to be. Although this novel is less of a social expose than is *Red Harvest*, it still portrays San Francisco as so corrupt that readers today have to be informed that Hammett actually understated his case. Herb Caen, a columnist for the San Francisco Chronicle, has recalled that in those days "The Hall of Justice was dirty and reeked of evil. The criminal lawyers ... used every shyster trick. The City Hall, the D.A., and the cops ran the town as though they owned it, and they did .... San Francisco was a Sam Spade city." (Quoted in William F. Nolan's Dashiell Hammett.) Counselor-at-law Sid Wise and District Attorney Bryan, characters in Falcon, give us some idea of what Caen (and Hammett) knew about Frisco in the Twenties, but actually Hammett goes easy on "the cops" and uses none of the other lurid aspects of the city that Caen describes (the rampant prostitution, public gambling, "rolling" of customers in the bars, for example).

CRITICAL RECEPTION

What Hammett and his editors had been waiting for was recognition that he was a literary novelist first, a mystery writer incidentally. And now Gilbert Seldes, a leading critic, wrote that "*The Maltese Falcon* ... is a novel and it is also a mystery story - the combination is so rare that probably not half a dozen good examples exist between *The Moonstone* [1868 classic by Wilkie Collins] and the present one.... The publishers quote someone as saying that ... Hammett has done for the mystery story what Dumas did for the historical romance. I consider that a ... justifiable ... comparison."

THE GLASS KEY

Hammett's fourth novel appeared serially in *Black Mask* even while Falcon was still being reviewed, from March to June 1930; Knopf issued *The Glass Key* in book form in 1931. Here Hammett returns on a big-scale to his **theme** of political corruption but adds the **theme** of male friendship.

MOVES TO HOLLYWOOD

In 1930 Warner Brothers released a vaguely recognizable film version of *Red Harvest* called *Roadhouse Nights*, and in 1931 David O. Selznick signed on Hammett as a screenwriter for Paramount. He moved to the movie colony. His first original film story, "After School," which he wrote in one weekend, became the basis for City Streets, starring Gary Cooper and Sylvia Sidney. For Universal, Hammett worked on Ladies' Man, which starred William Powell as S. S. Van Dine's detective, Philo Vance, and then wrote, expressly for Powell, an original Sam Spade story, "On the Make," released later as Mister Dynamite. And RKO produced a film version of Hammett's short story "Woman in the Dark."

With huge sums of money rolling in, Hammett hired a chauffeur, entertained starlets and writers lavishly, flew back and forth from L.A. to New York, and won a reputation at the studios as one of the writers (like Faulkner) most likely to show up drunk, if at all. Coming out of a five-day drinking spree, Hammett met Lillian Hellman, a 24-year-old book reviewer and manuscript reader. They became friends and lovers, off and on, for the rest of his life. He helped her learn to write; he critiqued and edited her plays, occasionally writing a scene himself to show her how; she became one of the leading playwrights of the century.

THE THIN MAN

Perhaps her biggest writing lesson came in watching him compose his fifth novel, *The Thin Man*. "Life changed," she said. "The parties were over … I had never seen anybody work that way; the care for every word, the pride in the neatness of the typed page itself, the refusal for … two weeks to go out even for a walk for fear something would be lost."

The Thin Man (1934) is quite unlike the earlier Hammett works. The hero is Nick Charles, a retired detective lured by his wife Nora into tackling one more case. In the Charleses, Hammett created one of the most loving married couples in American literature. This was Lillian teaching Dashiell how to write about women, about a trusting and tender relationship. "The thin man" is an inventor whom we never meet: He disappears before the book opens.

WORLD WAR II SERVICE

Forty-seven years old when Pearl Harbor was bombed, World War I veteran Dashiell Hammett tried to enlist again but was rejected because of his tuberculosis, his rotten teeth (all that smoking and drinking!), and his age. So he paid for his own dental work to meet Army standards, and when he applied again he somehow convinced the examiners that his lungs were better.

POLITICAL ACTIVISM

From his days as a Pinkerton, Hammett had been keenly aware of the struggle between workers and owners. Some critics see *Red Harvest* as a Marxist work, and Steven Marcus, in a famous essay published in the Partisan Review and used as an introduction to the Vintage book *The Continental Op* (1974), sees *The Maltese Falcon* as an allegory of the history of capitalism.

Hellman says that Hammett had many reservations about the Communist Party and never advocated "violent overthrow of the government." If he did join the CP late in the Thirties maybe as Marcus thinks, it was during the Party's "Popular Front" days when it welcomed anyone willing to fight fascism and Nazism: The irony is that no other American party was willing before Pearl Harbor, and so an antifascist like Hammett might well have joined the American left for that reason. In 1937, he was active, e.g., in raising funds for the Spanish Republic, then in a death struggle with the rebellious General Franco, who was supported by Hitler and Mussolini. A poll at the time showed that only two major American writers did not support the Spanish Republic.

POLITICAL CRISIS

After his discharge from the Army, Hammett taught creative writing at the Jefferson School of Social Science. Headed by Dr. Howard Selsam, who had lost his professorship at Brooklyn College because of his open Communist activities, the Jefferson School was dedicated to "Marxism as the philosophy and social science of the working class." In 1946 Hammett became head of the Civil Rights Congress, a group officially tagged as subversive by the Department of Justice. Three years later the Congress put up bail for eleven men convicted of "conspiracy to teach and advocate the overthrow of the government by force." When four of them failed to surrender to serve their prison terms, the court asked the CRC bail-fund trustees to identify the people who had put up the bail. The trustees, including Hammett, refused, were cited for contempt of court, and sentenced to six months in jail. (Probably one of Hammett's reasons for refusing to name the contributors is that people who put up bail for unpopular political figures are often persecuted by the community. For example, persons who put up bail for black activist Angela Davis were driven off their farm, and their children were driven out of school, during her trial in California in 1972. Accused of aiding prisoners who tried to shoot their way out of a courtroom, she was acquitted of all charges.)

When Hammett was released in 1952 from the Ashland, Kentucky, Federal prison and arrived in New York, he looked so feeble that as soon as Lillian Hellman saw him at a distance, she fled in horror. In 1953, Senator Joseph McCarthy interrogated Hammett about his books ("Have you ever engaged in sabotage?") and decided that they should be withdrawn from all U.S. libraries overseas. They had already been removed from 300 embassies when President Dwight Eisenhower decided that they posed no threat and ordered them put back. And so now Americans abroad and their friends are still allowed to read *The Maltese Falcon*.

LAST DAYS

Hammett's World War I tuberculosis had developed into World War II emphysema and into Cold War lung cancer. Penniless, an invalid, he spent his last four years as Lillian's house-guest in Manhattan, his last ten days in the hospital, his last two in a coma, dying on January 10, 1961. As a veteran of two wars, he was, at own request, buried in Arlington National Cemetery.

LASTING INFLUENCE

Five years later, the political winds having shifted, his publishers started bringing out new editions of his work. By 1972 his entire oeuvre - including selections of his short stories edited by Steven Marcus or Lillian Hellman - became available in a uniform paperback edition. In the Eighties critical studies and biographies began to appear at the rate of more than one a year.

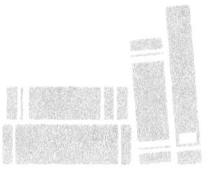

THE MALTESE FALCON

TEXTUAL ANALYSIS

CHAPTERS 1 AND 2

CHAPTER 1: SPADE & ARCHER

Function

The opening chapter of a novel, like the first scene of a play, is expected to establish the setting, or place, as well as the time-period of the action; to introduce some of the characters and show how they relate to each other; and perhaps even to launch the action by indicating the ways one or more of them are in trouble, in conflict, off-balance. Let's study in detail how Hammett, a veteran fiction writer when he starts TMF in 1928, handless these expectations as he opens his third novel.

Chapter title: suspense

Hammett gives his first chapter a title that not only names two persons but links them with an ampersand (&), indicating that this is a business partnership. Thus when the action begins with only one partner present, we wonder, in the back of our minds, how the absent partner will complete the picture -and when. From here on Hammett never misses a chance to create curiosity and suspense.

Setting

Hammett uses a classical technique employed by Homer and most story-tellers ever since: He describes his setting piecemeal, gradually, only as the characters move about and function within it. Thys we discover, first that Sam Spade is in an inner office; then, that his secretary works in an outer room, a reception area; we learn there is a neighboring office when we hear noises from it, and an outside court when we smell ammonia fumes coming through an open window; we learn only when Spade's visitor mentions it that we are in San Francisco; when he walks her out, we discover that an outer door opens on a corridor; we know finally that the setting will expand at least to other parts of San Francisco because Archer and Ms. Wonderly, characters we've already met, and Thursby, a character we haven't met, are all supposed to be at the Hotel St. Mark later that evening. Hammett never describes anything in the environment until a character comes to it or talks about it. Notice that he will use this highly economical and functional way of establishing the setting throughout the novel. A good example: We do not learn, until Spade stares at it in Chapter 3, that Archer has a desk of his own in the same inner office!

Diction: "hard-boiled"

The vocabulary that Hammett and his characters use includes colloquial terms and slang of the kind not found in the polite fiction of the day. In Chapter 1, for example: Spade tells Effie to "Shoo her [Wonderly] in," an expression he probably would not like the new client to hear him using at this point in their relationship. To shoo is to make the sounds and gestures that get animals or fowl to move along. Effie describes Wonderly as "a knockout," new slang in the Twenties for a beautiful or handsome person. Archer uses the phrase "cover up," slang to describe an attempt to conceal something scandalous or criminal. Spade warns Archer not to "dynamite" Ms. Wonderly. In the advertising profession (Hammett's earlier), to "dynamite" people is to lure them with misleading or garish language; to truckers, a "dynamiter" is a driver who abuses his rig through hard, fast, roughshod driving. Spade's use of "dynamite" to denote harsh, insensitive courtship of a woman sums up his opinion of Archer's attitude and approach. Hammett's use of down-to-earth, everyday, "street" language is one of the hallmarks of his new "hard-boiled" fiction.

Plot structure: defined

Generally speaking, the fiction writer so structures a story as, first, to arouse our curiosity and, then, gradually, to fulfill or satisfy that curiosity. In the short story there usually is time for only one such cycle of arousal and satisfaction. But in the novel the author may raise many successive questions, create several puzzles-some major, some minor - and resolve them in a series of answers, the most important questions and puzzles of course being answered or solved last. In Chapter 1 we are left with such questions as: Who is Thursby? Who, really, is Ms. Wonderly? What will happen when she meets Thursby and Archer spies on them?

Three plot patterns in Chapter 1

Within this larger framework of arousal-and-satisfaction, Hammett structures his opening chapter-definitely a "creation-of-curiosity" chapter-by using three reliable, traditional patterns of narration. (1) In detective fiction, the story often opens in the detective's office or home when some stranger appears to hire the private eye to help resolve some mystery or to protect someone in danger. (2) In the romances of knights-and-ladies the story may open when a damsel in distress appeals to a knight for help, or some lady of the king's court assigns him a mission.

Hammett's detective-knight is Sam Spade; the client-damsel is Ms. Wonderly whose problem, she says, is to rescue her 17-year-old sister from a certain Floyd Thursby, apparently a dangerous seducer and hoodlum.

But Hammett uses original variations on these first two patterns. Sam Spade's detective-partner and fellow knight, Miles Archer, immediately takes the mission away from Sam. And Ms. Wonderly will prove to be no helpless damsel, no innocent victim of the forces of evil. Her real identity and history, though, are the biggest long-range questions of the novel, the ones to be answered last.

(3) More general, more basic in nature than these first two story-patterns is the narrative pattern of arrival and departure. The chapter begins just before Ms. Wonderly's arrival and ends soon after she leaves. This is psychologically satisfying because it is one completed action yet it foreshadows and precipitates further-ongoing and incomplete-action.

Irony

Hammett consistently uses **irony:** that is, he plays on our concern with the difference between appearance and reality. The best and simplest instance in chapter one is an example of verbal **irony**. When Spade says to Archer, "You've got brains, yes you have," we sense Spade is saying one thing but meaning another. Other examples so far are instances of one form of dramatic **irony**, that is, a reversal of expectation. As we see a relationship developing between Spade and his new client, we feel-we almost hope-that he will handle the case himself; it is something of a wrench to us when Archer takes it over and Spade accepts that. The deepest, longest-range **irony** in the chapter of course consists in the appearance Ms. Wonderly creates here that will prove to be one of many covers for her real identity.

Characterization: Spade's tag name

Even before we see and hear Sam Spade in action, we have important clues to his character because Hammett has given him a tag name (see "Techniques of Characterization"). A spade is a sharp tool for digging, a good tag-name for a detective engaged always in digging for the facts. A spade is also a certain black figure, shaped like an inverted heart, printed on playing cards in the suit of spades. Is it accurate, though, to think of Sam Spade as really blackhearted? Is he really a man with his heart "not in the right place"? Is he a player in a game of chance? His last name also calls to mind our expression to call a spade a spade meaning "to tell it like it is," to avoid euphemism and roundabout expression. Will Spade then prove to be candid, blunt, direct, always avoiding circumlocution? Does Hammett prepare us to see Spade as always trying to be a good detective, that is a detective, - as the expression goes - in spades? Tag names not only characterize, they create suspense. To what extent will Spade live up to his name?

Characterization: Spade's looks

A tag-name alerts us to certain traits we may find in the character so named. So do his/her looks. Hammett's description of Spade's facial features as all variations on a "V motif" suggests a great convergence of lines, a pointing or concentration of all his powers. These inverted triangles all add up to one triangular face that suggests the cutting end of a broadsword or a pointed spade. Hammett's conclusion that "he looked rather pleasantly like a blond satan" alerts us to a kind of moral ambiguity/ambivalence. Western (especially Anglo-Saxon) culture conditions us to expect satans to be darkhaired, angels to be blond; to expect plainclothesmen to be virtuous or at least moral-not satanic-people. Will Sam Spade prove to be some combination of good and evil? Is some unethical use of a detective's powers already hinted in Spade's reassurances that they can "manage" the truant sister and "handle" the dangerous Thursby? Notice that Hammett does not describe the rest of Spade's physique until he stands up and we can see it. (This is analogous to the way Hammett handles the details of time or place-he doesn't describe any of them until they become involved in the action.) And then Hammett achieves another remarkably compact description, one that employs another geometric shape: "The rounded slope of his shoulders made his body seem almost conical-no broader than it was thick - . . . ." Spade is thus memorably pictured as a V-face poised on a cone-torso-somewhat streamlined, like a machine or even an automaton?

Characterization: Spade in action

Hammett's structure of the chapter allows him to characterize Spade, who is onstage continuously, as he interacts with three other characters, each with him only part of the time. With his secretary, he is playful, mock-flirtatious; she in effect informs us that he is a womanizer when she tells him he'd want to see Ms. Wonderly even if she were not "a customer." With the new client Spade is gallant, patient, attentive, sympathetic but businesslike as he hears her reasons why she wants. Thursby shadowed, and maybe confronted, by a detective. (Does he believe her story? Hammett, the good story-teller and practical psychologist, waits until Chapter 4 to reveal why Spade didn't "exactly" believe her.)

We are impressed by the intelligent, professional, succinct summary of her story that Spade gives his partner when he arrives. When Spade winks at Archer he indicates that he too thinks she's "a knockout" but his signaling Archer to be less obvious in his attentions shows that Spade is more discreet, less coarse, than his partner. If he is annoyed that Archer assigns himself to Ms. Wonderly's case, without consulting Spade, Spade doesn't show it. We soon learn how well he can conceal his real feelings. Perhaps he is biding his time, confident Archer doesn't have a chance with Ms. Wonderly on the personal level. At chapter's end Spade shows again that he thinks little of Archer's intelligence when he says sarcastically, "You've got brains…."

Characterization: Effie

Hammett quickly characterizes her, in appearance, as a tomboy and, in behavior, as a loyal and lively admirer of her boss, with whom she can be candid and casual. She functions in the action here as a contrast for Ms. Wonderly, who is more noticeably "a girl," and as a mirror for Spade, whom she can criticize freely. Her last name-Perine-is also the name of the outer coating that protects a grain of pollen, a fair name for the person in the outer office who protects her boss from intrusions.

Characterization: Ms. Wonderly

Following his detective's penchant for incisive observations of people's appearance, Hammett gives us his third such description in little more than a page of action. Notice that he makes Ms. Wonderly womanly in ways not even touched on in his sketch of Effie: the new client is "pliantly slender, without angularity anywhere," full-lipped, "high-breasted." Hammett signals her deliberateness in the way she dresses: in shades of blue and red to enhance her cobalt eyes and red hair. Her nervousness, blushing, embarrassment, trembling and lip-chewing all seem to grow out of her story of her sister's running away with an unscrupulous man (later we'll realize the real reasons for her shyness and stammering). Why is it so important to her that no mere anonymous detective, but rather one of the partners himself, must shadow Thursby? She betrays herself as having unacknowledged motives when she offers ten times the money necessary (in the Twenties $200 would have engaged a detective for two weeks: she offers that for a few hours' work!). Her unlikely name also teases us with questions. Is she like(-ly) a wonder? Doesn't she wonder too much? Is she wonderful? The name sounds so public-relations-ly that we won't be surprised to learn, in Chapter 4, that she has made it up.

Characterization: Archer

He seems unlikeable from the very moment he feigns surprise that Spade is in private conference with a woman. After all, wouldn't Effie have told him so? Archer continues to earn our dislike as he stands over Ms. Wonderly and ogles her with his "little brown eyes" until Spade has to warn him to desist. Again, he is as discourteous to his partner as he is to the client: When she wants one of them to shadow Thursby, he doesn't even discuss the case with Spade first but rather assigns himself to the job. His smug attitude at chapter's end-that he has won out over Spade in a competition for Ms. Wonderly!-deserves Spade's contempt for Archer's low intelligence.

Characterization: Thursby

When Spade asks Ms. Wonderly what Thursby looks like, we realize her answer is important to us for two reasons of a critical nature: (1) It shows us how Hammett's own experience as a detective influences his ability to provide superb descriptions of people's looks. (2) It illustrates one of the methods of characterization we have discussed earlier. For her description of Thursby characterizes her as well as him. Notice that she came well prepared to describe him and that she makes him sound so truculent and rabid that we wonder if and why she exaggerates. Notice too how Hammett can make each character absolutely distinctly different in appearance: In Thursby's case, this includes his athletic, military (combative, in the context of her opinion?) appearance, the cleft in his chin, thick eyebrows. Notice finally that Hammett has Wonderly use a very human way to describe Thursby's height: Hammett has her say he's as tall as Spade himself.

Point of view: behaviorism

We are now in a better position to understand the point-of-view problem we discussed earlier. By the point-of-view question we mean: From what point of human awareness is the action observed and related? Of several options open to him, Hammett chose for TMF the point of view of the author as limited And as objective narrator (parts of two options combined). That is, he would limit the scope of his story by telling it mainly from the point of view of one character, the hero, Sam Spade; but he would further limit it by observing Spade's actions only from the outside, as an objective observer would watch and hear Sam: an observer never privy to Sam's inner thoughts until Sam himself divulges them, an observer never commenting or intruding himself on the action.

Notice how Chapter 1 bears this out. In effect, Hammett follows Spade with a camera and a tape recorder. Spade is the only character always on stage, always the center of the action. Offstage action comes to our attention only when Spade learns about it. As we shall soon see, when Sam sleeps, there is no action onstage (with one interesting exception, to be discussed later).

Notice how this point of view-of the author as objective narrator-perfectly suits the aims of Hammett's "hard-boiled" fiction. Through his externalizing of the action he reduces the importance of the inner life-of introspection, reverie, fantasy-which is revealed to us only in the ways it affects the outer life. As Hammett practices it here, "hard-boiled" fiction is the literary equivalent of behaviorist psychology. Introduced by J. B. Watson in 1913 (just a few years before Hammett began to write), behaviorism seeks to explain behavior entirely in terms of observable responses to environmental stimuli.

CHAPTER 2: DEATH IN THE FOG

Title: double meaning

With the key words in his chapter title Hammett puts the emphasis on fatal event, blurry setting, and resultant suspense. The word Fog proves to have a double meaning: one literal, one metaphoric. First it denotes a physical fog: the clammy mist that shrouds San Francisco and even penetrates into Spade's apartment. By chapter's end it also connotes an all-enveloping psychological fog: the mysteries surrounding the deaths of Archer and Thursby; the two policemen's suspicions that Sam avenged Archer; the haze of ignorance, puzzlement, and anxiety that hangs over all three detectives.

Setting

Hammett continues to use the classical technique of setting the scene that we discussed earlier: He never describes anything in the environment until his main character comes to it (or he or some other character talks about it). Since the chapter opens in darkness, the only sense clues we get are sounds: telephone ringing, bed springs squeaking, something falling, "a man's voice." Not until the person making these sounds turns on the light do we discover that it's Spade and it's his apartment. Like a movie cameraman, Hammett follows his hero from his apartment to the Stockton Tunnel area of Frisco, to an all-night pharmacy, and back to Spade's place. We discover the complicated details of the Stockton area-e.g., the fence that Archer broke as he fell through it, a "notch between boulder and slope" where his body came to rest-only as Spade looks at them, one at a time. It's the setting, then, that provides closure for this chapter, which begins and ends with Sam in bed.

[N.B. (1) Alcatraz Island-from which originate the moans of the foghorn that reach Spade's apartment-is at the time of the action a Federal prison only for the military. (2) Dundy tells Spade that Thursby was shot four times "from across [Geary] street, when he started to go in [his] hotel." Frisco's Geary Street is a very wide thoroughfare. Anyone who could hit Thursby "from across the street," with a .44 or .45, was a very good marksman, given the inaccuracy of small arms of that caliber at such a distance.]

Plot patterns

Hammett adheres in Chapter 2 to several classical patterns in structuring his plot: with his own variations, of course. Most important is that his hero gets into serious trouble, his situation becomes more complicated, he is now definitely off-balance. A second classical development (in detective fiction) is that the official police and the private eye are plunged into their traditional rivalry as they both work on the same case; this conflict is intensified here because the police have good reason to believe that Spade has had good reason to avenge Archer's death. A third classical aspect: The murders are committed offstage, a practice common in ancient Greek drama and sometimes practiced in modern times. A fourth classical aspect of the chapter structure is that once again Hammett achieves closure in the action. Whereas he structured Chapter 1 to begin with Wonderly's arrival and to end soon after her departure, he patterns Chapter 2 to begin with Spade's leaving his bed and to end with his returning to his bed.

Plot complication

Hammett weaves an intricate pattern of complications, some talked about by the characters, many left to the reader to realize. Hammett begins the complications with the mystery of Archer's murder: the traditional whodunit? But other questions proliferate. Why is Archer's gun still in his pocket-why wasn't he ready to defend himself? Why does Spade refuse to go near Archer's body, why does he rush off, why does he not want to see or even talk to Archer's widow, Iva? Why doesn't it occur to him that his quick exit from the Stockton area will arouse the suspicions of the police? What happened to Ms. Wonderly, whom Thursby was supposed to visit? and Archer supposed to shadow? Notice that only Spade knows she was to be with Thursby, but not even Spade knows whether she was also at the scene of Thursby's death. Is it Ms. Wonderly, or Effie, or Iva about whom Sam says "Damn her!" when someone rings his doorbell?

Notice the clever trick Hammett uses when Spade elicits from the detectives the fact that Thursby had lived alone at his hotel: Only Spade and the reader know as a result that Ms. Wonderly's story of sister Corinne's being with Thursby is highly unlikely. Notice too that we don't know where Spade went right after he left the drug store. Is Dundy correct, then, in his assumption when he says he wouldn't blame Spade much if he had avenged his partner's death? Again, notice that Spade is alone in his apartment from 3:40 to 4:30 a.m.-have you wondered what he's been thinking about during this time? And have you noted that Archer and Thursby were not killed with the same gun? Prompts us to wonder why Archer's killer left the weapon on the scene. . . .

These questions-many of which we have had to infer ourselves, since Spade is not talkative and his thinking is not revealed to us-are just a small example of the reasons why Hammett's fiction is considered to be such a good tonic for the reader's logical and imaginative powers.

Characterization: Spade

In Chapter 2 Hammett finds the right occasion to complete his description of Spade's physique and shows him under severe pressure for the first time, stress from which Spade emerges temporarily safe and seemingly the victor in a grim game of one-upmanship.

In Chapter 1 Hammett described Spade as he looked fully dressed for the business day. In Chapter 2, when Spade is awakened in the middle of the night, we can catch a glimpse of his body after he doffs his pajamas and before he redresses. Hammett finds the perfect simile for Spade's thick body: it's "like a bear's," a simile Hammett then comically modifies because Spade is not hairy: "like a shaved bear's."

Thereafter Hammett relies on close details of Spade's facial expressions and voice to let us know how Spade feels (or wants others to think he feels). When Spade mutters "Damn her" in response to the street-doorbell, "a dull flush" takes over his cheeks; but when Spade hears men's footsteps, his face brightens and his eyes no longer look harassed. Later, Spade smiles at Dundy's warning that he might be caught doing something illegal; then Spade's eyes become "narrow and sultry" as he demands to know exactly why the police are intruding on him. At another point Hammett reveals that Spade can create a facial expression to conceal his real reactions: The wariness goes out of his eyes and he makes his eyes dull with boredom. Note how this ties in with our earlier comparison of Hammett's literary approach with the psychological approach of the behaviorist school: Both minimize the importance of the inner life, which is revealed to us only in the way it affects the outer life: in the way the organism responds to environmental stimuli.

In spite of his wariness, Spade in portrayed as no superman: he makes his mistakes, big and small. He set himself up for the police's suspicions when, at the Stockton scene, he refused to tell Tom Polhaus much about Thursby and refused even to look at Archer's body close up, making off instead-as the police now hypothesize-to kill Archer's killer. Then he unfortunately proposes the toast "Success to crime," meaning, probably, "How would we detectives make a living without it?" and not aware that they hear it, probably, as a toast to Spade's own success as a killer.

His apartment makes it clear the Spade is a man of modest means, engaged in dangerous work for little financial reward; his behavior indicates he is a loner, he keeps his own counsel, he fences well under stress, he is stoic and proud; he values self-control and dignity.

Characterization: Polhaus

Immediately on introducing each character (i.e., when that person first comes into contact with Spade), Hammett quickly distinguishes him/her with a few memorable details of his/her appearance. In Tom Polhaus' case, it's his "carelessly shaven dark jowls" and the implied contrast between his bigness of height and girth and his smallness of eyes. Tom clearly likes Spade (he's delayed dispatching Archer's body until Sam can view it) and he's hurt that Sam won't confide in him as much as Tom deserves. Tom seems loyal to Sam, but Sam seems to take Tom for granted. Tom dislikes the role he's been thrust into when he has to tell the lieutenant about Sam's haste in getting away from the scene of Archer's death and Sam's refusal to tell much about Thursby. Tom suffers from both Sam's intransigence and Dundy's long-lived suspicion of, and hostility to, Spade.

Apparently nothing would please Tom more than seeing the three of them combining their talents in their common cause.

Characterization: Dundy

In Lieutenant Dundy's case, the "memorable details" are a square face in a round head, short graying hair on lip and scalp, and a secret-society lapel pin (Masonic?). He is a type in detective fiction: the official police officer out to "get" the private eye. He has come truculently prepared to trip Sam up on several matters, all of them adding up to circumstantial evidence that Sam killed Thursby in vengeance for Archer's death. Stalemated by the clever Sam, Dundy concurs at chapter's end in a ritualized standoff: what Hammett brilliantly sees as a ceremonial shaking of hands.

Other characters

Most of the "extras" - like the policeman who challenges Sam's right to be on "Burrit St." and others who nod to Sam - function mainly to show that Spade is a well-known figure in the police world, while other people working in the dark serve to indicate that this a large-scale operation.

Diction

As a leader in the "hard-boiled" school of detective fiction, Hammett lets his characters use the language of their trade: Archer's heart is his "pump;" the bullet that punctured his pump is a "pill;" to arrest Sam would be to "pinch" him; to be following Thursby for detective purposes is "to be tailing" him.

Metaphor

As we've already seen, Hammett relies on a **simile** to describe Spade's body: it's "like a bear's," and he makes the real Frisco fog serve as a symbol for the psychological fog that settles on the three detectives. In addition we can see another feature in the landscape as symbolic: The fence Archer breaks while falling down the slope is a grim reminder of the fragile boundary between life and death.

Hammett and Zola

The French novelist Emile Zola, in his advocacy of a Darwinian-type ("naturalist") novel, insisted on painstaking descriptions of man's techniques. Hammett's 100-word description of how Spade rolls a cigarette (fourth paragraph, Chapter 2) is a perfect example of naturalistic description. Zola's reason was that a scientific fiction should record the relationship between man's techniques and his chances of survival. But Hammett's description here goes beyond mere Zolaist **realism** and verisimilitude. It serves to create both character and suspense. It characterizes Spade as the kind of man who'd rather "roll his own" than pay more for readymade cigarettes, a man who takes pride in doing physical tasks well. And of course while Spade's rolling that cigarette, we wonder what he's really thinking about. Since we know very little about the phone call, or what Spade plans to do next, his slow, silent work on that smoke makes us more and more impatient for the next step. We soon come to associate Sam's rolling a cigarette with deep thinking. Later we'll see it as a Freudian symbol.

THE MALTESE FALCON

TEXTUAL ANALYSIS

CHAPTERS 3 - 6

CHAPTER 3: THREE WOMEN

The title could bode ill for Spade, suggesting as it does the Three Fates of Greek Mythology who were supposed to control the fate of human beings, Clotho was the spinner of the thread of life; Lachesis measured it out for each person; Atropos cut it when that person was due to die. With the appearance in this chapter of Iva Archer, we will have met the three women who determine much of the action and, to a great extent, Spade's destiny. By the end of this chapter we shall be able to see which woman corresponds to which Fate.

Functions of Chapter 3

(1) This chapter introduces onstage an important character, Mrs. Iva Archer, who has figured thus far only in the conversations of Spade, Dundy, and Polhaus. (2). It also expands the Frisco setting

and advances the action as both Spade and Dundy continue their separate investigations of the murders. (3) Except for a few emotional moments on Iva's part, Chapter 3 provides the contrast of relative quiet after the stormy dramatic tensions of Chapter 2.

Setting and structure

Again Hammett closely relates his setting to his structure. Spade's concerns (1) being in his office with Effie, (2) take him to the Hotel St. Mark to see the house detective, and (3) return him to his office and Effie: Again, as in Chapter 2, a pattern of presence in, departure from, and return, to a home base.

Hammett structures his action economically as he interweaves Sam's onstage doings with the offstage actions of others as they are reported to Spade: (1) Effie's report of the suspicious condition of Iva's clothes and bedclothes at 3 a.m.; (2) house-detective Freed's report that Archer was on duty in the hotel lobby before he was murdered; (3) Effie's reports that while Sam was out of the office, Dundy came to look at Spade's guns, and Wonderly called to give him her new address.

Characterization: Iva Archer

Hammett characterizes her partly through her own speech and action, and partly through Sam's and Effie's discussion of her, revealing to us that Sam has been the lover of his partner's wife. Iva seems to be unaware that Sams regrets their relationship, since she has even thought Sam might have killed her husband because of love for her. Hammett quickly distinguishes her looks with three memorable features; prettiness past its peak; body sturdy but exquisite; mourning clothes looking "impromptu." And in his characterization of Iva, Hammett surrounds her with suspense: Why did she tell Effie at 3 a.m. that she had been sleeping when Effie can see, from a quick inspection of her street clothes and bedding, that Iva has just come in and not been to bed Could Effie's notion that Iva killed Archer prove valid? Do the police, already suspicious of Spade, know that Sam is the lover of his partner's wife?

Characterization: Spade

Hammett reveals, entirely through dialogue, that Spade's relation with Iva has been so serious that she can ask him whether he killed Archer for their sake, and Effie can ask him whether he'll marry Iva now. Actually, Spade is now reluctant to receive or return Iva's embraces, and he moves around to avoid her advances. Notice that Hammett has just shown us, in the outer office, that Sam can be more affectionate with Effie than with his "lover"! But his not wanting Iva with him right now is probably motivated by more than just his loss of interest in her: We can infer that he probably fears what the police would make of their adulterous love. We can see too a weak side of Sam when, in reply to Effie's candid criticisms of his "playing around" with Iva, he says that "that way" (he must mean sex) is the only way he can relate to women. Notice the **irony** throughout-for he is relating very well to Effie, who is jealous, apparently, of women to whom he relates "that way."

Unsuccessful in romance he might be, but he is surely effective in his work as, for example, he takes precautions with house-detective Freed to see that as few people as possible are involved in the investigation, he burns Effie's memo about Wonderly's new address, and he follows up on it at once.

Characterization: Effie

This plain woman, we now realize, has had to suffer contrast with two beautiful women: Iva as well as Wonderly. Effie is loyal to her boss, patient with his complaint that she hasn't kept Iva away, earns his praise for her deduction that Iva lied about being asleep, and gives him the benefit of her candid criticism: "… you're too slick for your own good." But we can fault Hammett in his characterization: He develops Effie as Spade's "girl Friday," feeding every macho boss' fantasies about having a female assistant whose sole ambition in life is to be allowed to slave for him, and love him forever, without hope of requital. (Friday was the name Robinson Crusoe gave to a grateful native who became his faithful servant.)

Three women

We are able now to identify the three women more specifically as the Three Fates. In addition to controlling the thread of life for human beings, the Fates were supposed to be the Triple Moon Goddesses. Clotho the spinner was the maiden goddess of the new moon and of spring. Lachesis the measurer was the mature goddess of the full moon and of summer. Atropos the cutter was the crone-goddess of the old moon and of autumn. By age alone at this point, the three women in Spade's life are Effie-Clotho, Brigid-Lachesis, and Iva Atropos.

CHAPTER 4: THE BLACK BIRD

Title

This chapter's title seems to be our first reference to the bird of the book's title. And Hammett might have intended a double meaning. Ms. Wonderly has recently come from Hong Kong, and Mr. Cairo originally from the Levant (lands around the eastern Mediterranean). In this expanding world that Hammett creates in this novel, it is not far-fetched to read even a Polynesian meaning into "The Black Bird." The title would refer then not only to Cairo's "statuette" but also to Spade himself. For in the South Seas "blackbird" is the slang name for a native (a Kanaka) who has been kidnapped for use or sale as a slave-laborer. Certainly Spade is captured in the surprise ending of Chapter 4, and this captivity is a brief **foreshadowing** of a longer state of captivity in a later scene.

Characterization: Spade

In this chapter Spade's troubles mount and multiply as he faces conflicts on every level: psychological, moral, legal, and physical. In each of his four encounters-with Ms. Wonderly (now Ms. O'Shaughnessy!), Sid Wise, Effie, and Joel Cairo-he reveals still another aspect of his character. In his dealings with Brigid O'Shaughnessy, he seems first in calm control as he explains that they never believed her story (about her sister and Mr. Thursby) because she paid them more than she'd had to for such a simple problem. But then Spade is perplexed and even angered as he faces a really knotty problem. As we know from Chapter 2, Dundy has an urgent legal right to know the name of the client Archer was working for when he was shot. But Brigid wants Spade to protect her from (1) police investigation altogether, and from (2) her other enemies as well: all this on faith because she can't yet divulge the real nature of her problem!

As soon as he takes Brigid's money and is committed to helping her, it's clear he knows he's in legal difficulty because his next stop is his lawyer's officer. His conversation with Sid Wise convinces us that Spade is an old hand at shady practices. Not only does Sid remark that Spade's been in worse legal predicaments than this one, but also they go off together to see "the right people." With the arrival of Cairo in his office, Spade goes on in this fourth encounter so far in this chapter to reveal more about himself. His using the same introductory approach with new client Cairo as he used with new client Wonderly/O'Shaughnessy indicates that Sam likes to use certain bland routines automatically as a way of covering his real thought processes. Notice that this proves to be valuable when he says nothing to Cairo's suspicion of a connection between the two murders.

Characterization: Brigid

Effie's insistence that "That girl [Brigid] is all right" is a good reminder to us that when we knew as little as Effie knows, we thought the same. Brigid is definitely revealed now as an unethical, scheming, manipulative person who poses as a shy and weak woman in need of masculine protection. One of the finest moments in the novel occurs when Spade again calls a spade a spade: When he lets her know that her getting down on her knees, her tearful appeal to his "strength and resourcefulness and courage" to rescue her from her dangerous situation, are all just so much play-acting. He's even able to tell her that it's her eyes and the throb in her voice that make her a good actor!

Look at the risk this crafty woman takes in calling his bluff and acting as if she has to go on without his help. He can-legally, he should-go to the police with incriminating facts about her. How can she be so sure he'll change his mind and continue on the case after all? Maybe his little charade-putting on his hat and making ready to leave-is his way of letting her know the price will be high, because he's hard to get and because he'll be facing the same kinds of dangers Archer and Thursby faced.

Characterization: Effie

Why does Sam ask Effie what she thinks of Wonderly/O'Shaughnessy? Is he still trying to make up his mind about Brigid? In any event, as Effie cautions Sam about his treatment of "that girl . . . in trouble," we get the definite impression that Effie has been the conscience of Spade & Archer. She is capable of getting angry at her boss - and embarrassing him with her moral rectitude-when she thinks he's at fault. **Irony:** While she may be right about how Sam could "bleed" Brigid, she is wrong in saying "That girl is all right, and you know it." Both Sam and the reader know better now. Surely one of Hammett's motifs is that character judgments are difficult if not impossible.

Characterization: Cairo

Hammett loads the dice against this man. Even before he enters Spade's office, Effie has characterized him as queer. Then Hammett describes him as effeminate (as though that's bad): fleshy hips, pampered hands, a mincing walk, all the stereotype clues that he's gay. Hammett tag-names him Cairo to strengthen the picture of him as Levantine, that is, a person from the Levant, the eastern half of the Mediterranean world. (Levant means rising: the East is where the sun "rises.") Hammett completes his portrayal of the Levantine by having him wear a perfume made from oils and resins and named after Cyprus (in French, Chypre), an island in the east Mediterranean.

The Levantine often appears in literature as a person part French or Italian who serves as a commercial middleman between Europeans and Near Easterners. For example, he appears in T. S. Eliot's The Waste Land as "a Smyrna merchant," also homosexual, who is intended as a symbol of degeneracy. Hammett was not enlightened on matters of sexual choice, but neither was Freud himself in the Twenties.

Hammett expects us to infer, from Cairo's questioning of Spade that Cairo suspects there's a connection between Thursby's death and Archer's, and that is why Cairo has come to see Archer's partner.

CHAPTER 5: THE LEVANTINE

Diction: "hardboiled fiction"

When Cairo puts two serious questions to the private eye, Spade answers with two slang terms that had come into common use at the time of the action. When Cairo complains "... why did you strike me after I was disarmed?" Spade mockingly replies that he was embarrassed to find that "that five-thousand-dollar offer was just hooey." A slang synonym for nonsense, hooey entered the language of the streets suddenly in the late Twenties. When Cairo wonders why Spade risks serious injury to prevent Cairo's searching his office if the black bird "is not here," Spade protests that he can't just let anybody "come in and stick me up. . . ." This slang phrase-meaning to rob a person at gunpoint so that he sticks his hands up-had become common American English around 1915.

Chapter 5 as a duel

This brilliant and dramatic scene develops with the physical precision of a duel between swordsmen, and with the mental depth of a game between chess players. Let us analyze this conflict first for its physical aspects, then for its psychological features, and then sum up with what the duel has revealed about both characters.

Physical techniques

Hammett, as we have already noted, writes in the Zolaist (or naturalistic) fashion when that suits his purpose. And he is a Zolaist when he focuses on the techniques Cairo and Spade use in their physical encounter. He gives us in fact almost a slow-motion account of the duel.

Apparently Cairo's assumption is that if he stands behind Spade and holds his gun in his left hand against Spade's back, he can prevent Spade from interfering with his search of both Spade's clothing and his office. Why doesn't this plan work? Notice Cairo's mistakes. He has told Spade to clasp his hands together at the back of his neck. And so when Cairo reaches around to pat Spade's chest, he is right under Spade's outstretched right elbow. If he had told Spade to "stick 'em up high!" that elbow would now be too far away to come into action so fast.

Spade has obviously practiced this kind of maneuver, bringing the elbow down hard on a gunman's jaw, pinning Cairo's foot with his own right heel, whipping his body around so he can disarm Cairo with his right hand. Hammett describes this action as if Spade is a dancer. And Hammett describes Spade's follow-through-when he stiff-arms Cairo unconscious with one blow to his cheek-as if Hammett is a machine in motion.

Hammett devotes about 350 words to demonstrating how Spade's technique undoes the results of Cairo's technique and more than reverses the situation. Both Hammett and Spade then take their time -another 300 words, is it? - as the private eye goes through another well-practiced routine: a methodical, detailed search of the contents of Cairo's pockets.

Psychological techniques

From here on Hammett stages a battle of wits between two topnotch minds. It's not an easy feat for an author to create two first-rate mentalities in opposition. Consider the high points:

Spade's search. Hammett's point of view in this novel suspensefully deprives us of access to Spade's thoughts, but we begin to see, soon after he completes his search of the contents of Cairo's pockets, that his wits are working as well as his fists. He correctly concludes (from addresses written on Cairo's hotel stationery) that Cairo has already searched Spade's apartment, that Cairo did not come prepared to make good on his offer of $5,000 for the "bird," and other things we'll realize later.

The "bird" in the office? Cairo reasons well that the black statuette must be in Spade's office because he risked death at gunpoint to prevent its being searched. Spade's witty answer hides what we can infer he's really thinking: Since there must be some connection between Cairo's and Brigid's goings-on, Sam has got to gain the upper hand to pursue it, maybe bringing these two people together so he can broaden the scope of the case (and earn fees from both of them).

Cairo's vulnerability. Spade thinks he has Cairo "by the neck" because if he turned Cairo over to the police they would see some connection between him and Archer and Thursby. Cairo counters suavely with the telling news that Spade's reputation shows he'd not help the police if he lost money thereby. Sam's accepting a "retainer" to help Cairo "recover" the "bird" for its "rightful owner" proves Cairo correct this time.

The "rightful owner." Spade uses Cairo's mention of the "rightful owner" of the bird as his chance to find out who else is involved. His wild question - "What about his daughter?" - seems to be based on a hunch that Brigid might be related to the "owner." At least the question has "stirred things up" - it strikes such an emotional chord in Cairo that he unwittingly reveals that such a father-daughter team is involved. And the question pays off too because it gives Cairo the idea that Spade knows more than he actually does.

The standoff. Spade seems to lose the final round in this battle of wits - or does he? Perhaps he has assumed that now he and Cairo have a business deal under way, he can give Cairo back his gun and that Cairo won't use it on him again. He's wrong but this time he can afford to laugh: He has his retainer, and he knows that Cairo won't find the statuette in Spade's office.

Notice that Cairo reaffirms the "business deal" by not taking back his $200 when he has the chance.

Characterization: Cairo

Ironically presented to us at the beginning as a weak fop, Cairo has proved to be a worthy rival for Spade especially on the mental level. Cairo takes pride in his style of dress as well as his style of speech. His ticket to the theatre suggests he has cultured tastes as well as a flair for language, and that he seeks diversion even in the midst of a dangerous enterprise. Hammett balances out these strengths with evidence of Cairo's weaknesses: a nervousness when carrying out a bold plan, a yielding to panic (but just briefly) when he's disarmed and being hurt.

Characterization: Spade

He proves increasingly talented in making useful deductions from the facts. He plays his hunches effectively. He has too a useful ability to suppress his own curiosity and to mask it with feigned indifference, to conceal the train of his thoughts. He can overpower a man with a gun as deftly in Chapter 5 as he rolled a cigarette in Chapter 2. He can joke in dangerous moments. While he prefers not to carry a gun, he gets an almost ecstatic satisfaction out of knocking a man unconscious with his fist. It seems to be a matter of pride in his technique but also the pleasure of a sadist.

An affinity?

Spade suggests that they put all their cards on the table. Cairo refuses. Nevertheless, when Spade laughs at the very end of the chapter, do you feel there is some kind of affinity between them? Is it simply that they agree that they need each other? Isn't it more than that? They are both players in the same game staged in the same grey area of amorality. As Diane Johnson says, in her brilliant Hammett, detectives and "their prey understand each other and are in a strange way comfortable with each other."

CHAPTER 6: THE UNDERSIZED SHADOW

Techniques: Zolaism

As both a writer of detective fiction and a Zolaist, Hammett gives us detailed descriptions of the techniques his characters use. Some of Spade's detective tricks are well-known in that profession, but his main tactic is really Hammett's invention. Well-known is Spade's trick for eluding his "shadow," the "youth" who's been tailing him for hours: Spade enters a large apartment house, presses the bell-buttons one after another until some innocent tenant buzzes the street-door open; Spade tears through the building and out a back door before his "shadow" can figure out where he's gone. Hammett's invention: The Continental Op, anonymous hero of several other Hammett stories, says that his basic technique is "to stir things up." This is what Spade has done in Chapters 5 and 6. Trying to figure out Brigid's relation to what Cairo calls "the rightful owner" of the black bird, he tries this: "What about his daughter?" Cairo is certainly rattled, as we have seen, so now Spade knows there is a father-daughter relationship in this case, even if Brigid is not part of it. Again, at a quiet moment in Spade's visit to Brigid's, he mentions that he has seen Joel Cairo. Brigid is certainly stirred up, revealing not only that she knows Cairo but even about the bird, neither of which has she told Spade about until now. Spade's master method, then, is to absorb new facts gleaned from one person and to try them out on another. Then, having established that they already know something about each other, he arranges a confrontation between them (as he does between Brigid and Cairo in the next chapter), picks up new facts, and uses them on somebody else. We could call it Hammett's chain-reaction technique.

Plot and conflict

These chain-reactions, then, develop Hammett's plot which thus seems to unfold in a natural, lifelike manner. What keeps us following these reactions, of course, is that they set up suspense and conflict. Hammett alternates his conflicts with quiet interludes. In Chapter 6, Hammett opens with just such a quiet session as Spade meditates at his desk. But as he goes from office to cigar-store to restaurant, suspense develops: Who is this youth who is "tailing" Spade? In retrospect, we can figure out that Spade realizes he has to lose this shadow before he goes to Brigid's, but if possible he must also try to identify him first. Hence his detour to search for Cairo, intercepting him at the Geary (remember the ticket to the Geary that Spade found in Cairo's pockets?). There is now some brief conflict between them as Cairo is upset that Spade has allowed "the kid in the cap" to see them together. But Spade proves he had to: He has to know whether "the youth" is on Cairo's side or on "the other side," just in case the situation becomes violent (suspense). Now another brief conflict as Sam eludes "the youth." Then a quiet period of banter at Brigid's before Sam drops his bombs about Cairo and his $5,000 offer for the bird. Major conflict now as Brigid is angry that Spade seems ready to work for Cairo instead of her, because Cairo can offer him more money, and Spade is angry that he has had to learn about these things not from her but from Cairo. Suspense: When she asks "Can't you trust me just a little longer?" we realize she really has been waiting for some other crucial event to occur before she feels she can tell all her secrets to Spade. **Irony:** He's finding them out on his own anyhow. Original twist to the plot: The detective has to find out on his own what his client should have told him, before he can help her. Resolution of this conflict: She realizes she must talk to Cairo, and Spade will soon have the confrontation he's been working for. New conflict: Iva is outside Spade's place when he and Brigid arrive and Iva's jealousy puts Spade in new trouble. New quiet: Spade and Brigid seem relaxed as they wait for Cairo's show to let out. Notice that the main action (stirring things up for Brigid) alternates between tension and relaxation and even with other actions (getting rid of first "the boy" and then Iva).

Characterization: Brigid

Spade's good news-that she will not have to face a police inquiry just now-seems to give her the energy and perspective to handle a whole range of problems with vigor, resourcefulness and insight. She turns his criticism of her play-acting into a merry joke. She communicates to Spade, under the guise of anger at the thought, that she will do anything to buy his services. She resolves the threat of having to compete with Cairo for Spade's loyalty by deciding that the three of them must meet. At the end she seems grateful that she has Spade to protect her during an interview she might not be able to handle alone. It is a tribute to Hammett's portrayal of the complexity of character that she now seems likeable.

Characterization: Spade

Each of the four encounters he has in this chapter gives us further insights into the strengths and weaknesses of a very complex character. He shows ingenuity in the way he handles the pint-sized "shadow," first leading him into a situation in which Cairo can decide which side "the youth" is on, then eluding him so that the youth can't follow Spade to Brigid's. Spade again shows his belief in casual violence as a solution to human problems when he talks of hurting "the youth." He allays, for the moment at least, Cairo's fears that Spade has erred in letting the shadow see them together.

By threatening to desert Brigid, to switch his loyalties to Cairo because the Levantine offers him more money than she possesses, and by taking a sort of down payment on her offer of sex, Spade maneuvers her into realizing that the next step is for her to confront Cairo under Spade's protection. Actually, we realize he has not intended to desert her because only if she has "the bird" can he get it to Cairo and collect the $5,000 reward. He needs both of them.

With Iva he reveals his cowardly side, his inability to be honest with her. In his relationship with her he doesn't have the decency or strength to call a spade a spade. Is she a mother-figure for him? Of his "three women," as we have seen, she is his "crone-goddess."

THE MALTESE FALCON

TEXTUAL ANALYSIS

CHAPTERS 7 - 10

CHAPTER 7: G IN THE AIR

Title

"G in the Air" is a pun-both verbal and visual-on "Air on the G String." That is the title that August Wilhelmj gave to his 1871 violin arrangement of a Johann Sebastian Bach melody. In music, an air is a melody, a tune. But the violinist, in moving his bow and fiddle through space, also plays "in the air." And so does Brigid when she traces "a swift G in the air" (to let Cairo know who had Thursby killed).

Setting

This is the first chapter staged entirely in Sam's rooms. Here we see the kind of apartment drama Hammett had in mind when he decided to exploit further the situation he had used in his short story "The Whosis Kid." This is a situation in which the conflict is intensified because it is compressed into a confining space. Conflict between Cairo and Brigid is staged in Spade's living room-bedroom; conflict between Spade and the two police-detectives is contained in a hallway! Suspense mounts painfully at chapter's end as the two policemen crowd into the room where Cairo and Brigid are already at war.

Structure: suspense, counterpoint, conflict

The chapter is divided into three parts; the structure is musical as well as dramatic. (1) In the opening scene, suspense is created when Spade reaches Cairo and invites him to talk with Brigid. While we're waiting for Cairo's arrival and the confrontation between Spade's two clients, Spade tells Brigid about one of his most meaningful cases: This little story serves as a kind of counterpoint to the ongoing action of the larger, overall story. Some conflict and further suspense are generated when Brigid presses the issue of "trust" and gets Spade to agree to let her handle the confrontation with Cairo in her "own way." (2) Conflict and suspense widen and deepen when Cairo arrives, upset by the presence outside of the "boy" shadow. But this conflict subsides briefly into relative quiet as Cairo and Brigid talk cautiously about the bird: she wanting to sell it, he pressing for more information. Meanwhile we are aware of the counterpoint of Spade's presence, the suspense in his listening, thinking, waiting to see things stirred up. Fierce conflict breaks out after Brigid taunts Cairo for his homosexuality and after Cairo taunts her over a boy she "couldn't make." Has Brigid provoked Cairo deliberately to force Spade to fight him?

(3) With the arrival of Dundy and Polhaus, the conflict and suspense mount sharply. Dundy's suspicion that Spade killed

Archer has been reinforced by his discovery that Iva and Sam had been lovers. When Sam won't let the policemen inside his apartment, (a) dramatic irony is generated because Dundy assumes that Mrs. Archer is now inside and finding her there would strengthen Dundy's hypotheses; but we know she's not there, although she wanted to be. (b) The irony is doubled because we know that what the police would find inside would be equally good grist for their mill. And what is going on inside is present in our minds throughout as contrapuntal action. When Cairo calls out "Help! Police!" (irony again!), the two strands of action become one as Spade is forced to let the two policemen into the now-crowded apartment. This chapter is a masterpiece of dramatic and contrapuntal structure.

The Flitcraft parable

But this chapter is famous not only for its dramatic intensity but also for the parable that Spade recites to Brigid and that she misses the point of. (A parable is a short story told primarily to teach a moral lesson. Most famous parables are those told by Jesus, e.g., those of the Good Samaritan and the Prodigal Son. Famous modern parables include those Kurt Vonnegut uses in his novel *Breakfast of Champions* and the parable Hammett uses here.) Actually Spade's parable teaches two lessons, and Hammett sets the two in conflict in Spade's mind and certainly in the reader's. Indeed the Flitcraft story serves as an epitome of Spade's philosophy and of the meaning of Hammett's fiction.

The first lesson is that the universe is governed, not by order and system as Charles Flitcraft had believed, but by blind chance, as he saw when the beam fell from a skyscraper and hit the sidewalk inches away from him. This lesson prompted Flitcraft to break out of his orderly family and business life and live haphazardly, in the belief that living randomly is living more harmoniously with Nature.

The second lesson is one that Flitcraft missed, ironically, but that Spade sees and profits by. After a few years of random rambling, Flitcraft unconsciously drifted back into an orderly life. Adopting a new name (a tag-name, like his original name, as we shall soon see), the new Charles Pierce married again, went into business again, and settled down into a new groove much like his old groove. The second lesson, then, to Spade at least, is that no matter how much the rest of the universe is run by blind chance, humanity must find order in life, even if this means deliberately imposing it on reality.

Spade and Flitcraft

The parable provides Spade with a reason for living, with a world-view. What could be more random, more chaotic than a murder mystery so complex as the Archer-Thursby cases? Even if history is replete with millions of unsolved mysteries, Spade must seek out the secret connections, the order in the facts of his cases. To extend the parable to Spade's detective work: He attacks a mystery by "stirring things up" further and watching the results; by creating more disorder in an effort to find some order.

[N.B. "Stirring things up" is the way Hammett's "Continental Op" describes this method. We shall hear Spade's own description of his "way of learning" in Chapter 9.]

Flitcraft's tag-name #1

To flit is to move quickly. A flit person is swift, fleet of foot. To flit can also, in some areas where English is spoken, mean to change one's residence. Hammett has invented the perfect tag-name for a man who learns the craft of flitting-only to unlearn it.

Flitcraft's tag-name #2: Pierce & Peirce

Giving Flitcraft his second tag-name of Charles Pierce is Hammett's way of alluding-with a switch in two letters-to the American philosopher Charles Sanders Peirce (1838-1914). Peirce's book *Chance, Love, and Logic* appeared posthumously (1923), as did his multi-volume Collected Papers (1931-1958). Peirce's philosophy ties in significantly with the Flitcraft parable and the Spade-Hammett philosophy in several ways.

(1) Peirce was a pioneer in the study of probability, which is one of the notions Spade and Hammett are concerned with here.

(2) Peirce coined the word abduction to describe a third method of reasoning (induction and deduction being the other two). In abduction, the investigator tries to figure out what circumstances could have led to the situation he is confronted with. This is such common procedure in detective work that it could only have reinforced Hammett's own ideas. But surely it might have attracted him to Peirce and helped establish in his mind an affinity between detective work and philosophy.

(3) One of Peirce's main theses is that the meaning of an idea is to be found in its consequences. Earlier we noted a parallel between Hammett's treatment of Spade's behavior and Watson's psychology, which teaches that inner mental processes should be studied only as they reveal themselves in action. Now we can see that Hammett's treatment of Spade's behavior-giving us nothing of his inner life except what he reveals in dialogue and action-has its parallel in Peirce as well as in Watson. The main

ideas of both philosopher Peirce and psychologist Watson were in print several years before Hammett wrote *The Maltese Falcon*. The conclusion seems inescapable that Hammett, a prodigious reader, studied either the original works of both thinkers or some popular writings expounding them.

(4) There is still another method of Peirce's that might well have given Hammett a philosophical basis for his own methods. Peirce actually revised his entire system of philosophy every time he discovered a new system of logic! This is analogous to what Spade (or any Hammett hero) does: With each new "stirring up," he reconstructs his explanations of the situation he is investigating. So, in Peirce's continual reconstruction of his systems of ideas Hammett might well have found at least a parallel to, a reinforcement if not the source of, his heroes' approach. For the overall message of Hammett's work is that not only in detective work but in all of life, reality is actually a series of different realities, each one an update on the last version, each a mental construct ripening for revision. For the investigator in any field, this is an important lesson about how to proceed, what to expect, how to relate to developments. In rebaptizing Charles Flitcraft as Charles Peirce, then, Hammett acknowledges his indebtedness to the real Charles Peirce.

Characterization: Cairo

He's beginning to lose the poise he has so valued until now. He suspects again that Spade might be the one who put a "tail" on him. He recovers sufficiently to conduct an intelligent interview of Brigid. They obviously know each other so well that she knows exactly which button to press to drive him berserk: She need only taunt him about his homosexuality. At this point there seems to be no further possibility of Hammett's two clients' working together. Is that what she wanted?

Characterization: Brigid

The Flitcraft parable is wasted on her. "How perfectly fascinating," she lies, and she's been so fascinated she can hardly wait to talk again about the pending Cairo visit. First she gets Sam to agree to let her handle it her way. Then she provokes Cairo first with a taunt and then with a slap, manipulates Sam into taking her side in renewed physical combat, and nets her possession of Cairo's little gun. Apparently she decided, sometime before or during the powwow, that she did not want to sell the falcon to Cairo. Perhaps she wanted to meet him (under Sam's protection) just to gather information, to see what Cairo already knew.

Characterization: Spade

This particular private eye proves himself on this night to be a superb practical philosopher and a good practical psychologist. His interpretation of the Flitcraft case, as discussed above, is insightful, a good statement of his own orientation. His sharing it with Brigid is a tribute to her intelligence, an act of love actually, maybe even a friendly warning. We shall have to look for ways he might think the parable applies to her. We also have in this chapter a sustained instance of how he stirs things up. While seeming to be an indifferent observer and listener-a broker interested only in bringing buyers and sellers together-what has he learned? The suspenseful point-of-view Hammett uses forces us to guess, to make inferences. Has Spade, in his slack tranquility, seen the "swift G" that Brigid obviously intended to be so swift he would miss it? Has Spade inferred what the reader can, that certainly Brigid, and maybe Cairo too, has served as a sexual decoy in enterprises they collaborated on in the Near East? Is Sam aware of the spot that puts him in, or is he, as Effie warned, "too slick for [his] own good"?

Similes: assessment

Within the Flitcraft parable-itself a form of metaphor-Hammett imbeds two unforgettable similes. Spade tells Brigid that Flitcraft disappeared from his first life "like that, like a fist when you open your hand." Spade says that when the beam almost killed Flitcraft, "He felt like somebody had taken the lid off life and let him look at the works." These two powerful figures of speech, plus two highly imaginative **allusions** (to Bach and Peirce), plus the stunning parable of Flitcraft, plus the apartment drama with its rapid dialogue ranging from inquiry to insult; all combined make "G in the Air" a masterpiece of modern fiction.

CHAPTER 8: HORSE FEATHERS

Title and diction

In 1930 even hardboiled fiction was too respectable to use "obscene" four-letter words. Hence Hammett employs the euphemism "horse feathers," everyone knowing that what is really meant is the term no writer would hesitate to use today: Horse shit. As Dundy speaks the phrase, it is an expression of both incredulity and disgust over Cairo's ingenious but farfetched explanation of how he acquired the gash in his forehead. This euphemism was coined by William ("Billy") De

Beck in his classic comic-strip, "Barney Google." And of course, the Marx Brothers increased the coinage.

Sam uses two slang terms, one - "sap" - centuries old, the other - "bulls" - a late nineteenth-century coinage. "Sap" is a short form for "saphead," or a person stupid, foolish, or easily duped. "Bull" means a law-enforcement officer of any kind (prison guard, uniformed policeman, plainclothesmen, etc.).

Plot complication

This chapter further complicates several of the story elements. The conflict between Spade's two clients has reached a stage of serious violence, with Sam in greater danger from that quarter. What began as traditional rivalry between police-detectives and the private eye has also reached a major crisis as Dundy, furious at being continuously outwitted by Sam, hits him: We are to see this as a serious breach of professional ethics. Even though Dundy's mistake puts Sam "one up," he has new problems: The police know now not only about his relationship with Iva, but also about Brigid. And there's the "boy" outside. Are the troubles unleashed by "stirring things up" multiplying faster than the benefits? By no means the last complication in Sam's situation, the romantic element, is also moving toward a crisis. Will Sam respond to Brigid's sexual gambits? Why has she made them? Why would he respond?

Theme: overlays of reality

Right after our discussion of Hammett's Peircean concern with reality as a series of realities, he supplies us with a superb example of the phenomenon (or na) in this chapter. First (1) we have Brigid's account of what happened while Sam was out of the room, then (2) Cairo's account, then (3) Sam's explanation of what was "really" going on; we have to take into account the extent to which those three stories differ from (4) what we know happened; we know too that soon (5) Brigid will be asked by Sam to tell him what really happened, and that, no matter what she says, (6) Sam will construct his own version.

Characterization: Brigid

Although she continues to play the role of a frightened girl, she also continues to be a tough manipulator of other people, able to thrust and parry with the most unexpected developments. To appreciate her swordswomanship, we need only remember that the police need to know who Archer's client was and here she is, exposed to the police in a situation where a chance remark-by Cairo, for example-could reveal her true identity. She picks up her cues fast from Spade: As the first to laugh, she supports Sam's explanation that the tableau of violence has been staged to "kid the bulls."

If Cairo is telling the truth, why would she have told him that she and Sam plan to murder him as soon as the three are alone again?

Characterization: Cairo

While Brigid plays the frightened and helpless girl, Cairo seems more and more like the boy victimized by every adult. But Brigid is not a comic figure, and Cairo certainly-from the moment he, a criminal, shouts "Help! Police!" to the moment he decides it's better to leave with the police than stay with two adults who have whipped him repeatedly-Cairo certainly is emerging as a tragicomic figure if not a full-fledged comic. And when he calms down (how do you do that with blood streaming from your forehead and lip?) he displays an impish sense of the comic. He joins in the hoax Spade is perpetrating on the police, providing a vaudeville-pratfall explanation of how their little charade miscarried and he hit the floor with his brow. All that's missing from his part of the kidding is the banana peel. He is completely at home in the criminal world, enjoying the battle of wits if not the physical risks. He is one of the criminal characters making us realize that their world is Sam's too.

Characterization: Spade

In addition to noting the new complications Sam faces (Plot Complication above), we should appreciate his nimble ingenuity as it is displayed in this scene. Notice that he does not speak much at the very beginning, apparently "sizing up" the situation. His "blinking sleepily" is one of his ways of looking withdrawn and uninterested but he soon takes control of the interactions of the four other people in the room, assigning them their places in a scenario he has just composed. Consider how claiming that Brigid in one of his operatives solves many potential problems: It conceals her real address from the police and gives her the same immunity from police interrogation that Sam has. Claiming that the whole incident was staged to make fun of the "bulls" is another stroke of genius. Notice that its success depended on Sam's knowledge of Brigid and Cairo: specifically that they would be able to take their cues quickly and act out the scenario as a good escape from Dundy's plan to run them all into jail. The **irony** is an essential part of Hammett's message: even enemies can join forces against a common enemy; or, allies may not be what they seem to be. Finally, notice Spade's footnote to his Peircean philosophy: If reality is really a series of changing realities, we might speed up the process by inventing some realities as a means to an end. His explanation to the police of what they have blundered into is no less plausible, no more absurd than the truth.

Style: irony

Irony is the very soul of literature. If a writer can't invent ways of exploring the difference between appearance and reality he can't compose good fiction or drama. This chapter abounds in both forms of **irony**: verbal (a situation in which someone says one thing but means another; or says more than one knows) and dramatic (a situation in which what we expect is replaced by the unexpected, or one in which we watch how a character functions in ignorance of the facts which we are privy to). Thus Polhaus calls Brigid "sister" to emphasize that he does not feel brotherly toward her; Cairo says that Spade told them the policemen would understand the hoax because they are "friends of his;" a police officer in the right is provoked into committing a wrong; a gun moll becomes a private detective; enemies join forces as a tactic; a story that is a total fabrication resolves the situation.

CHAPTER 9: BRIGID

Function

After the fast, stormy action of Chapter 8, which involved five excited people at cross-purposes, Chapter 9 provides a contrast of relative-even domestic-quiet, involves only the two main characters, and advances mainly the romantic element in the plot.

Title: irony: pun

As a chapter title "Brigid" has three meanings. Aside from the fact that it declares the chapter to be (1) about Brigid, it is also (2) ironic. Brigid (Bridget, Brigit, etc.) was an Irish goddess of fire, fertility, and wisdom, later associated with an Irish Christian saint. To make certain we get the ironic Irish connotations, Hammett gives Brigid the last name of O'Shaughnessy. Only as (3) a pun does the name "Bridge-It" ring true (i.e., non-ironic) for her: She bridges the gap between Sam and the criminal world; at chapter's end she effects a sexual bridge between them.

Characterization: Brigid

What is the meaning of her uneasiness when she is alone again with Sam? We can infer that her close brush with the police reminds her that she is more dependent than ever now on Sam. Whenever he becomes displeased with her, he can change his story (i.e., create a new reality) and turn her over to the "bulls." Her first reaction is to act again like a frightened child, appealing to paternal feelings she should know by now Sam doesn't have. Her next reaction is to admit she's afraid of "two men," Cairo and Sam, with the implication, apparently, that the latter must reassure her and protect her from the former. She needs now to make him more dependent on her, and this surely must be the first reason she sets about to seduce him this night. Her joking about the gang's getting the falcon from the Russian general clearly implies that her part was to seduce him, one of several reminders she gives Sam of her sexuality. The second reason she embraces him is clearly to end his persistent interrogation. As we shall see in the opening scene of the next chapter, he has his own reasons for returning her embraces.

Characterization: Spade

Hammett reveals four important things about his hero in this short chapter. (1) He is capable of passionate rage. He has suppressed so much of it in the confrontation with Dundy-being forced to take a cowardly blow to the chin-that it takes five minutes for him to give vent to it. Perhaps Hammett errs here in making Sam's outburst almost a mechanical thing (Newton's law: Every action triggers a reaction equal in force and opposite in direction). But we must keep in mind that Hammett is working under the influence of the behaviorists, whose S-I-R (stimulus, integration, response) formula is considered mechanistic by non-behaviorists. (2) Again, Hammett makes it clear that to Spade, the end justifies the means. (a) To force Brigid to stay so he can interrogate her again, he lies about the "kid's" being outside. (b) To prepare the way for his next morning's work, he yields to her sexual advances. (3) As Lesson Two in his explanations to her of his method (the Flitcraft parable was Lesson One), he says "My way of learning is to heave a wild and unpredictable monkey-wrench into the machinery." (4) Hammett finally shows us that Spade is capable of sexual tenderness too, even if it proves later to be more tendentious and deliberate than spontaneous and loving.

Style: sexual imagery

Hammett uses several devices to create a sexual atmosphere. Sam uses a knife to slice a slender loaf of bread while Brigid idly caresses the body and barrel of a pistol. All three items are considered to be basic phallic symbols. Indeed, in the right context, laying food out on a table can symbolize sexual readiness. While Brigid wonders how to end Sam's questioning, she pulls her skirt down over her knees, body language that (unconsciously or no?) draws attention to her loins. Meanwhile Sam has been rolling a cigarette, now clearly revealed as a phallic symbol: until now this ritualistic act has emphasized his lonely need, but in this context tonight, it takes on overtones of successful arousal.

CHAPTER 10: THE BELVEDERE DIVAN

The title: setting

The title focuses the spotlight on a seemingly unimportant piece of hotel furniture which is, however, of great tactical importance to both "the youth" and to Sam. As Hammett says twice in quick succession, it's the "divan from which the elevators could be seen." It becomes also the simple setting of Spade's first face-to-face confrontation with "the youth" and of Spade's reconciliation with Cairo.

Diction

In 1930, we noted earlier, not even the "hardboiled fiction" writer was allowed to use four-letter words considered obscene. Hammett finds in this chapter a neat way to mock this censorship by showing that the reader will know exactly what "the boy" is saying when Hammett describes it as "two words, the first a short guttural verb, the second 'you.'" Half a century later, anyone old enough to be reading the Falcon has already heard "Fuck you" so often in the movies alone that its shock value is fading. But at the time of the Falcon action (1928) "the boy" uses such talk (along with "Shove off" and "Jack") to show he's tough and even belligerent.

Allusion: irony

When the frightened Brigid (hand on a gun) cries out: "Who is that?" Sam answers with a veiled allusion: "Young Spade bearing breakfast." She gives no sign that she understands the irony in his thus paraphrasing a line from the Roman poet Vergil: "I fear the Greeks bearing gifts." He enjoys the secret pleasure of telling her she should fear him without telling her. For the reader Sam's allusion sums up the meaning of his stealing her key and searching her apartment while she slept: The sex was, in part at least, a means to an end.

Characterization: the youth

In keeping with his realistic way of describing places and people, Hammett has waited until Sam sits a foot away from "the boy" to give us our first closeup of the young gunman. Hammett has thus built up to the horror of a creature not yet twenty, face beardless and sickly white, eyes that focus on places below yours, lips in a perpetual sneer, and pockets bulging with "tools." Hammett creates one of his innumerable "dramatic moments" when Spade finally ruffles "the boy's" sneering poise by acting as if Sam knows all about "G" and "the boy's" connection with "G." Actually, we can infer that Sam respects the boy's professionalism in his reaction to Sam's disappearance into the apartment house. We are to infer from Sam's deduction from the newspaper account that the boy very intelligently (if wrongly) assumed Sam had entered the apartment house to see Brigid and, again intelligently, the boy searched apartments identified on the "vestibule-register" as belonging to women. We can infer too now that "G" has linked Brigid as well as Cairo with Spade.

Characterization: Cairo

The psychological affinity between the criminal mind and the detective mind is again dramatized as Cairo and Spade-who just hours ago were locked in physical combat-see this as no firm barrier to their resuming their working relationship. Indeed, the criminal has found it advantageous, during the "grilling" to "adhere to the course indicated earlier" by the private eye. By now we should remark too that Cairo is a man of literary style in his speech. No matter what kind of situation he's in, he speaks ironic, well-turned sentences, as we hear when he wonders whether to talk again with Sam: "Our conversations in private have not been such that I am anxious to continue them." Then, capitulating, he adds: "You have always, I must say, a smooth explanation ready." But Hammett characterizes Cairo as a smoother talker than Spade is.

Characterization: Brigid

Note well that she is already using the new power that she thinks their new sexual relationship has given her over Sam. It's now her latest, most sanctimonious excuse for refusing to discuss the bird: "You can't ask me to talk about that this morning of all mornings." Note too that her continuous play-acting limits her understanding of what's really going on. Having used the sexual relationship for her ulterior purposes, she still does not see that Sam is using it for his. She does not suspect, apparently, that it is Spade who has searched her apartment and has thus, among other results, manipulated her into moving where, he probably hopes, he can keep a better eye on her (as well as Effie's eye).

Characterization: Spade

Manipulation seems to be one of Hammett's main themes; In American life success depends on psychological manipulation of people hour after hour. Take a look at the action in those terms. In the very first paragraph we realize one reason he has made love with Brigid: To get her hotel key and search her rooms before she wakes up. Though he doesn't find the bird, he does find a mysterious rent receipt (the importance of which we will not learn about until the last chapter). Next we realize that he did indeed catch that "G in the Air" and now he's using it as one of his "wild, unpredictable wrenches" to throw at "the boy." Next he manipulates the house detective into throwing the boy out for reasons only we (not the detective) can imagine: To get him out of the way before Cairo comes back and walks into the boy's purview (why else is the boy at the Belvedere?). Next he manipulates Cairo into understanding why Spade has to side with Brigid if Cairo is to get his falcon. And when Sam gets back to his office he already knows Brigid is there: He knew his ransacking of her apartment would drive her there asking for help. All that's left is for him to manipulate Effie into manipulating her mother into hiding Brigid at her house. Sordid? It isn't even lunchtime yet. Sam's day has just begun.

THE MALTESE FALCON

TEXTUAL ANALYSIS

CHAPTERS 11 - 15

CHAPTER 11: THE FAT MAN

Title

This chapter is appropriately named after one of Hammett's most extraordinary portraits, perhaps his most masterful description of a physical type. After Hammett published *The Thin Man*, these two extreme-opposite types became mythic figures in American fiction, film, and radio drama.

Contrast in drama types

Again Hammett makes artistic use of contrast, this time in two types of drama. The first scene is subtle psychological drama; the second turns into unsubtle melodrama: i.e., exaggerated emotional behavior calculated for stark effect.

The first scene opens with a dramatic misunderstanding, with Sam acting as if his surprise visitor, Iva, has come to apologize for her conduct the night she saw him with Brigid. Actually, ironically, she has come (1) to apologize for something worse, for making an anonymous and spiteful call to the police that night, and giving them a phony tip that they'd find Archer-murder-case evidence at 891 Post Street: Iva's jealous way of trying to interrupt his sexual liaison. She has come too (2) to warn him that her husband's brother has also been to the police with his suspicion that Sam murdered Archer in the hope of marrying Iva. Sam's disentangling the misunderstanding and getting to the facts is handled with consummate psychological realism.

By contrast, the second scene mounts quickly into bombastic histrionics as Sam, impatient with loquacious Gutman's failure to say anything real, furiously gives him a deadline for opting in or out of the falcon deal, and exits with the incredibly hammy line: "Five thirty - then the curtain."

It's not Hammett writing corny melodrama. It's his hero's faith in wrench-heaving.

Litotes

By now we should also comment on Hammett's occasional use of litotes (pronounced lie-to-tease), a figure of speech in which we affirm something by denying its opposite. For example, when we want to say "Pretty good!" we might actually say "Not bad!" Litotes is a form of understatement. When Spade remarks that he took it for granted Brigid was lying, Gutman adds: "That was not an injudicious thing to do."

ingratiating and a flatterer to the point of offense. He has a ready supply of supposedly reassuring and complimentary remarks:

"You're the man for me, sir . . . I do like a man that . . . We begin well, sir. . . ." He is unaware that some of his **cliches** are ridiculous: "You're . . . a man cut along my own lines" is no compliment coming from a gross explosion of body. But one of his ready-made remarks does underscore one of the **themes** of the novel: "I don't trust a man who says he's not looking out for himself . . . he's going contrary to the laws of nature." Who in the novel is not so looking? Polhaus, most likely; Effie, possibly.

Gutman's dress-cutaway coat and striped trousers-is an unwitting comic commentary on his pretentiousness, on his hypocritical conformance to the fashions dictated by the "best" people.

Characterization: Spade

Hammett the psychologist has so structured the chapter that we can see that Spade's fury directed at Gutman and "the kid" is really an accumulation of fury that began with Iva's infuriating visit. But some of Spade's tantrum is calculated. The closest he comes to literally heaving a wrench is heaving a glass. These guys are so accustomed to violence that Gutman doesn't even look at the mess. Notice that Spade signaled his mounting anger with a clever, timely, sarcastic repetition of Gutman's original toast: "Here's to plain speaking and clear understanding." Notice finally here the strongest indication yet that Spade sees as one of the privileges of the private eye his right to take the law into his own hands: "Keep that gunsel away from me . . . [or] . . . I'll kill him."

Characterization: Iva

In this chapter she strengthens our impression that s a "sticky" personality. She clings and cloys. Either beca she senses he no longer loves her, or because she is he incapable of real love, she stirs up situations that willy- produce at least some kind of passionate experience. N that she is the only one in the relationship who keeps refe to his love for her, and that she keeps saying he won't fo her as though that's what she really needs: To go on suffe He is of course responsible for fueling her masochism. N now the increasing dramatic **irony** in her plight: Now it's necessary than ever that she not be seen with Sam. And sh about her whereabouts the night of her husband's death though she has suspected all the time that Sam learned the from Effie. A major contrast between her and Sam: Her ov and provocations keep her miserably off-balance. His giv some desperate momentum and direction.

Characterization: Gutman

His last name is both a literal and an ironic tag-name. Th syllable "gut" draws attention to his huge belly. The ful is an English approximation of the German for "Goo(His first name is also ironic: Caspar was one of the Thr bringing gifts to the infant Jesus. Add to this the nai Hammett gives to Gutman's choice of hotel (Alexandria) have in this chapter, too, strong associations with the Ne

Here Hammett creates another tragicomic figure. is all flourishes and verbal furbelows. He talks big al need to talk but all he wants is answers to his questio

CHAPTER 12: MERRY-GO-ROUND

The title is based partly on Sam's own explicit use of the phrase but it has its implicit meaning too. Referring to Iva's "merry-go-round riding" the night of her husband's death, Sam is describing her three trips to his place to no avail: The carousel takes you nowhere. Referring to Brigid's disappearance as "another merry-go-round," he must be thinking that his sending her off in a cab has also been "to no avail." He does not say it out loud the third and fourth times, but note that his going to the taxi-stand, and then to Gutman's, both for the second time within hours, adds up to four merry-go-round events in one day. Going nowhere except in circles can itself be seen as ironic, but the phrase is also ironic here because none of these four cyclings is merry.

Diction: "gooseberry lay," etc.

With complex overtones, Sam uses an old American slang expression when he taunts "the boy" with: "How long have you been off the gooseberry lay, son?" In nineteenth century hobo talk, a "gooseberry" was a clothesline with clothing hanging on it. Taking the clothing was as easy as picking wild gooseberries; a hobo expedition with such results in mind was called "a gooseberry lay." By extension, the phrase came to mean any safe, easy criminal job. So Sam's first insult suggests the boy has only recently (or not at all) quit easy jobs and is now trying for big ones. But of course Spade, a rabid anti-homosexual, also uses the phrase with what he thinks are insulting sexual implications. In some editions, the word gooseberry has been omitted.

Other usage: When Wise tells Sam that Archer was "raging" his wife Iva by telling her he had a date with a girl at the St.

Mark, Wise means Archer was teasing, taunting her. This use of "to rag" is now obsolete. But when Iva thought Miles was "just trying to get under her skin," she was using a slang term still popular today. The metaphor here is the comparison with a tick that burrows under the skin of its unwitting human host.

Structure: suspense

This chapter draws much of its air of mystery and suspense from the fact that three of its four main events come to us second hand, at one remove from the story's present reality. From Wise, Sam hears how Iva spent the fateful night of her husband's death (corroborating Effie's charge that Iva was not at home that night); from Effie he hears that Brigid's cab ride did not take her to Effie's house; from the cabbie Sam hears that Brigid bought a newspaper and then changed her destination to the Ferry Building. And these developments are left in limbo for the time being because Sam must now keep with Gutman the appointment Sam himself demanded.

Characterization: Spade

If we needed any evidence to prove that Sam Spade is no Superman, no ideal hero, Chapter 12 provides more than enough. We can think of at least eight adjectives of a pejorative nature to apply to his behavior in this chapter:

Fallible. He has missed a valuable clue. Reading over the Call to see what it was that diverted Brigid from her taxi-ride to Effie's house, he passes over the "Shipping News." After all, after reading the Call Brigid told the cabbie to stop at the Ferry Building, in those days at the center of shipping activity in the

Frisco harbor. Why has he missed the connection? Working too hard?

Sexist. When Sid tells Sam how jealous Iva spied on her husband, Spade says "Jesus, these women." [Jesus is omitted in some editions.] This is a remark adversely critical of all women on the basis of gender alone.

Unethical. He sends Iva to a lawyer, then forces the lawyer to violate professional confidence and tell Sam what Iva confided. Sam believes that the end justifies the means.

Insulting. He rewards his lawyer for his extraordinary cooperation by telling him that the only honest lawyer is a dead one.

Manipulative. He manipulates everybody to do what he needs. Two examples: He tells the cabbie reluctant to talk that they can clear this first with his employer if he insists. This would cost the cabbie some fares; he cooperates. Spade reminds a lawyer reluctant to violate a professional confidence that his detective-client Spade brings a lot of money into the lawyer's accounts; the lawyer cooperates.

Scapegoatist. He tries to make Effie the scapegoat for Brigid's disappearance: "...let's do something right."

Self-pitying. When Sam's lawyer complains about Sam's mistreatment of him, Sam says: "I haven't got enough to think about. ...What did I do? Forget to genuflect [kneel] when I came in?"

Sadistic. Browbeating Effie and Sid isn't enough. When he beats up the gunman, he enjoys it. Note that "A soft light began to glow in his yellowish eyes" just before he violently disarms "the boy."

Justification? The pragmatist philosophy Sam espouses (pragmatism was founded by Charles Peirce: See our analysis of "G in the Air") might justify Sam's attitudes and actions on the grounds that he is efficient and effective. His unhesitating heaving of many a wrench into the machinery produces results. It is true that he is working under enormous pressure in extremely complicated circumstances. "Now I've got to remember to be polite," he complains to Wise. Hammett is building up Spade's bad temper as a way of speeding up the action as it rises to a resolution.

CHAPTER 13: THE EMPEROR'S GIFT

Title

"The Emperor's Gift" is a grand title and an ironic one. Grand because the Emperor turns out to be Charles V, the greatest of all the Hapsburg emperors (1519-1558). As Holy Roman Emperor and as King of Spain he controlled Spanish America (his forces completed the conquest of Mexico and Peru), the Low Countries, and parts of Italy and the Austrian lands. The title is also ironic because the emperor's grand gift turns out to be a curse.

Gutman's story: corrections, additions

"These are the facts," Gutman says of his account of the black bird. But he romanticizes, embellishes, and simplifies to suit his purpose. For example: (1) The "yearly falcon" was not the only rent the Hospitalers had to pay for Malta. They had to agree to defend Tripoli from the Muslims, a costly obligation. (2) The "first year's tribute" was not the "glorious golden falcon" but indeed "an insignificant live bird." It was only as their wealth multiplied that the Knights of Malta substituted "jewel-encrusted statuettes." And yes, there was more than one such falcon: it had been one a year once they decided to give statuettes. (3) Gutman is fuzzy on the exact lands Charles V rented to the Malta Knights: They were given the islands of the Maltese archipelago (Malta, Gozo, Comino) plus the job of defending Tripoli (on the African mainland). They didn't like this at first because they found the islands "barren" and the people "savage," but their dislike softened as Malta proved a good headquarters for preying on the Saracens and their wealth.

Allusions

Most of Gutman's allusions to his sources are given in sufficient detail so that you could, if you wished, track them down. One off-hand allusion perhaps deserves elaboration here. "These are ...historical facts, not schoolbook history, not Mr. Wells' history, but history nevertheless," Gutman says. This was an important allusion when *The Maltese Falcon* appeared in 1930. H. G. Wells, famous science-fiction writer (*The War of the Worlds; Invisible Man*), had published in 1920 his *The Outline of History*, one of the great adult-education books of all time. Maybe Gutman is familiar only with Wells' shorter version, A Short History of the World (1922). Well into the Fifties, Wells' histories were assigned as background readings in college courses in the humanities.

Characterization: Gutman

Hammett continues to portray Gutman as a loquacious flatterer - "you're ... an amazing character" he tells Spade, as he regards him with "fond eyes"! - and a good manipulator of people and events. He proves to have an amazing memory for historical facts as he relates the story of the falcon (with a few errors, as we've noted). His obsession with the falcon takes on all the romantic fervor of a quest. And his quest is an ironic parallel to the Quest for the Holy Grail. Steeped in this pseudo-religious passion, Gutman sounds one of Hammett's main themes: "... the Holy Wars ... were largely a matter of loot;" that is, good and evil go hand-in-hand throughout history.

Once again Gutman, in spite of his sophisticated air, reveals himself as a man of prejudice, judging people by chauvinistic stereotypes. Just as he ridiculed Cairo ("That's the Greek for you") so he ridicules Kemidov (who had "the natural contrariness of a Russian general"). And in spite of his affectation of rationality, Gutman is properly ridiculed by Spade as a man whose "logic" is flawed by greed. Gutman first describes the falcon as "the property of whoever can get hold of it." That makes it Brigid's, Spade correctly infers. But Gutman contradicts himself: "No, sir, except as my agent." Spade says "Oh" with irony undetected by Gutman.

Wilmer and the plot structure

Hammett's narrative technique, as we've remarked earlier, is to describe or identify only when the action requires it. Thus we have not known that the "boy," the "kid," the "youth" is named Wilmer until Gutman has to summon him by name. Wilmer serves to frame the chapter. The main action is the one scene between Gutman and Spade, a scene that involves a story within a story. This scene is preceded by Wilmer's entering Gutman's apartment in a state of humiliation; it is followed by Wilmer's revenge as he kicks Spade in the head. As usual, Hammett achieves closure and containment in each chapter.

Metaphor, symbol, allegory

The fate of the falcon elicits from Gutman the appropriate metaphor that it "was a football in the gutters of Paris." The falcon already can be seen as a symbol of man's greed, from the time it was given to the Emperor as a sign of prosperity to the time Gutman has sent his "agents" after it. And Steven Marcus, a brilliant critic and writer based at Columbia University, gives the falcon both a symbolic and an allegorical meaning. Hammett, he says, "unwaveringly represents the world of crime as a reproduction in both structure and detail of the modern capitalist society that it depends on, preys off of, and is part of . . . *the Maltese Falcon* itself . . . turns out to be and contains within itself the history of capitalism. It is originally a piece of plunder, part of what Marx called "the primitive accumulation'; when its gold encrusted with gems is painted over, it becomes a mystified object, a commodity itself; it is a piece of property that belongs to no one-whoever possesses it does not really own it."

CHAPTER 14: LA PALOMA

Title

"La Paloma" is Spanish for "the dove" or "the pigeon." This is an ironic name for a ship that figures in a mystery about *the Maltese Falcon*. A dove is a symbol of peace; a falcon is a bird of prey.

Structure

Chapter 13 consisted of a simple structure, just one scene in a single setting. By contrast Chapter 14 has a complex structure, four scenes with eight places visited by Sam and one visit offstage by

Effie. As usual 14 achieves balance and closure. In scene 1 Sam and Effie discuss new developments; in scene 2 he makes his rounds of four hotels on foot; in 3 he makes his rounds by telephone, setting up his work for the rest of the day (foreshadowing); in 4 he and Effie discuss new developments. This efficient organization of the plot reinforces our general impression of Sam's orderliness and energy: he gets a lot done in a short time.

Diction

Sam wants Effie to find out from her professor-cousin whether Gutman's story is valid or is "the bunk." Until the mid-Twenties this word was slang for nonsense, lies, exaggeration, but by the time of the action "the bunk" is good usage. Sam also wants the professor to keep the falcon story "under his hat," that is, secret, confidential. When Luke the hotel detective sees Sam's forehead he says "…somebody maced you plenty." In 1930 "mace" did not denote what it does today: a spray of poison gas that one can use against an animal or a human assailant. Rather the word denoted a club, or a blackjack. The original mace was a medieval weapon, a club made of metal and/or spiked so that it could be used to penetrate armor. The "gladstone bag" Sam and Luke search in Cairo's room is a piece of leather luggage that opens flat into two equal compartments.

Characterization: Effie

Hammett continues to characterize her as the macho boss' dream girl, the female "Friday" who lives self-sacrificingly for and through her employer. Sam has obviously forgotten that he told her to stay on duty till he returned or called; she has done so, with a smile, all through the night; and now she doesn't get a word of thanks. Nevertheless she enters enthusiastically on the problem of verifying Gutman's story, probably grateful to have a chance to work on a professional level for a change. She functions plot-wise to get her cousin's verification and to bring the news-via a piece of soot on her nose, an ingenious comic touch-that La Paloma is afire.

Characterization: Spade

Chapter 14 deepens our knowledge of both his strengths and his flaws. His ability to dictate to Effie from memory what Gutman told him about the falcon is prodigious. (But with the low-key approach of hardboiled fiction Hammett simply attributes Sam's feat to Spade's training as an interviewer.) Then, from Sam's outward behavior we can infer he knows now he erred the day before when he could find no clues in the Call. When Cairo's having cut out a piece of the "Shipping News" shows him what he had overlooked, we realize he's lost 24 hours because he did overlook it. Notice that he keeps saying the wound on his forehead looks worse than it really is: His self-image does not allow him to accept sympathy.

Zolaist technique

Hammett's 100-word account of how a detective opens a door serves several artistic purposes: (1) It meets Zola's requirements for naturalistic reporting of the techniques people use to survive. (2) The details pile up neatly toward a climax (he smothers the sounds of the "other keys," fills his lungs so not even his breathing will be audible when he gets inside!) that proves to be a neat anticlimax: No danger inside, just Effie still on duty at 6 a.m. (3) This is perfect foreshadowing for a major buildup to an anticlimax in Chapter 19. (4) It further characterizes Sam as thorough, alert, always on the qui vive, and therefore sometimes ridiculous.

CHAPTER 15: EVERY CRACKPOT

Title: Synecdoche

The title is taken from Spade's defiant, insulting speech to the District Attorney at chapter's climax: He's tired of "being called things by every crackpot on the city pay roll." Crackpot means a person with a cracked head, someone erratic, impractical, even crazy. Here the word is a good example of synecdoche, a figure of speech in which a part represents the whole. Hammett has prepared us for this outburst when Sam complains to Sergeant Polhaus, just an hour before, about "every bull [policeman] in town working . . . to pile up grief" for him. Since the chapter consists of Sam's lunch with a policeman followed by an interrogation by the D.A.-two persons close to the underworld-we're not surprised that it contains the longest burst of underworld slang in the novel.

Diction

In giving Spade a report on what the police have learned about Thursby, Polhaus resorts to several slang expressions. That the gunman "knocked over" a row of stuss-games, was "turned up" by his "twist" and "sprung" by a gang-leader means Thursby robbed a series of card-game banks, was betrayed to the police by his girlfriend, and let out of jail because of his gang's political influence. That Thursby whipped a "twist that had given him the needle" means a girlfriend who had ridiculed him. Spade's calling Cairo a "lily" is a reference to his being a homosexual. The

D.A.'s saying Monahan "welshed" on his gambling debts means he failed to pay them off. Spade means, when he says Thursby "lost" Monahan, that the bodyguard allowed his boss to be killed. Sam's opinion that the information he could add to what Bryan knows would "poop" the D.A.'s theory (that Thursby's death was an instance of gangland revenge) means his information would dump excrement on it. And Spade's challenge to the D.A. to "pinch" him is an invitation to arrest him.

Structure

In order to help achieve realism, fiction (like drama) is structured to reflect the ebb-and-flow, or the advances and retreats, that we experience in real life. Chapter 15 is a good example of the pattern of ups and downs that Hammett creates. In the first scene, Hammett lessens the pressures on Sam. But Hammett's second scene greatly increases the pressures. Here's how: The lunch scene functions to show us Polhaus at his continual efforts to lessen the tensions between his boss and his friend, to let Sam know that it was Thursby's gun that killed Archer (i.e., Sam is no longer a suspect), and Cairo was not (as he told Sam) detained by the police "all night." The interrogation in the Hall functions to complicate Sam's problems, revealing to us that the D.A. thinks Sam guilty of withholding information about his secret client that would help solve the Thursby murder. So, in spite of Polhaus' efforts to make life easier for Sam, Sam is in worse trouble now.

Characterization: Bryan

Hammett's physical description of the D.A. features, as do all Hammett portraits, at least one unforgettable detail: "the over-large mouth of an orator." His actions indicate that he is also a bully. Flanked by his assistant D.A. and a stenographer, Bryan uses the pressures of numbers, legal threats, as well as innuendos in an effort to cow a single person who came without his lawyer. Typical of Bryan's tactics: he tries to put Sam off-guard by describing this as an "informal" meeting but later tries to intimidate Sam by saying that in informal as well as formal situations he is still the D.A. He expresses a cynical view of one of the very institutions he as D.A. should respect: the Fifth Amendment, which, as Bryan should know well, is in the Bill of Rights to prevent the authorities from extracting confessions by torture or other forces like threats and intimidation. He is supposed to know that a citizen's invoking the Fifth does not necessarily prove he is guilty, but Bryan hints that Sam might invoke it for that reason.

The D.A. is right: Sam is concealing something and could be risking a charge as an accomplice after the fact. (Only in the last chapter will we discover what he is concealing.) There is no doubt that if Bryan knew who Sam's client is, it would provide Bryan at least with information about Thursby's activities on the night of his death. But Sam does have to protect his client's privacy. We must admit though that by now he has personal reasons for shielding Brigid that he can't admit: He stands to make money as a broker in the falcon sale. And he doesn't even know where his client is right now.

Spade's flyting

The argument between Spade and Bryan reaches the intensity of a flyting. This is an exchange of personal abuse between two characters in an epic poem. At its peak the flyting results in at least one of the characters flinging out a wild boast about his intentions and his prowess. One reason he makes such a public declaration is that now he must live up to it. At novel's end we should look back to this flyting and see how well Sam has lived up to the task he publicly sets for himself:

> . . . my best chance of clearing myself of the trouble you're trying to make for me is by bringing in the murderers-all tied up. And my only chance of ever catching them . . . is by keeping away from you and the police, because neither of you show any signs of knowing what in hell it's all about.

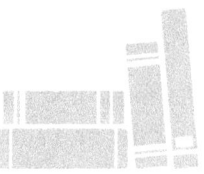

THE MALTESE FALCON

TEXTUAL ANALYSIS

CHAPTERS 16 - 19

CHAPTER 16: THE THIRD MURDER

Title

Hammett had been criticized for excessive violence in his earlier novels. It is possible that he titled this chapter to emphasize the fact that even this late in the story there have been only three murders! Readers who have not read *Red Harvest* and *The Dain Curse* might be surprised to hear that critics actually talk about "the lack of violence" in *The Maltese Falcon*. After all, we have witnessed some serious roughing up of Cairo and Wilmer, we've seen Archer's body where it tumbled to rest down a hill, and in this chapter we see a man die in agony. But that's a real "lack" as compared to the rivers of blood that flow in earlier Hammett works. They are replete with graphic descriptions of bullet holes and dagger wounds. Only in "The Third Murder" does the Falcon even approach those excesses. And "The Third Murder" is the only one in which the victim bleeds on stage: the actual shooting of Jacobi, like those of Archer and Thursby, occurs offstage. And Hammett will devote only a sentence or two to the fourth murder.

Structure: ebb and flow

After the dramatic conflict between Spade and the D.A., Hammett gives us the contrast of a quiet respite: Chapter 16 opens with Sam's doing a few routine chores. But conflict rises again as Effie intimidates Sam into resuming his search for Brigid. A reluctant Sam resolves his own inner conflict by going to La Paloma to pick up Brigid's trail. Again there is a reversal of mood as Sam returns cheerful, presumably ready to report some success. But he is interrupted by the news that Cairo has returned to his hotel, and Sam gets there too late: failure, setback. More suspense develops as Sam tells Effie what he has learned from La Paloma's crew, this account then interrupted by the mounting sensationalism of the appearance of the dying sea-captain. The chapter ends with renewed suspense: Can they keep the police/D.A. ignorant of the precious prize that Jacobi delivered? Can Sam get it to safety before the people who shot Jacobi can shoot Sam?

Simile, metaphor, litotes

The mounting tension in this chapter evokes from Hammett a series of superb figures of speech. Perhaps because Sam had hoped to cage Cairo, at least briefly, Luke tells Sam "Your bird has fluttered." Hammett's colorful description of the dying man includes three similes. He is so tall, his coat so long, it is likened to a "sheath" and later called "tubular." Using his hands not to break his fall but to protect the falcon, "he fell forward as a tree falls." There the corpse is as "still as the floor it lay on." The statuette is "black as coal." There is one more excellent example of litotes in Sam's account to Sid of his visit to Bryan: "Well, we didn't kiss when we parted."

Irony

The presence of the falcon becomes the occasion too for irony. Hammett says that Spade's "widespread fingers had ownership in their curving," an ironic reference back to Spade's ironic comments on Gutman's ironic double-standard in defining ownership (Chapter 13). And Effie has to point out (screaming) to Sam that he is actually stepping on Jacobi's corpse: In his greedy gloating over the bird he has unwittingly violated the respect for the dead we/she normally expect to see observed. The tableau of Sam's stepping back on the dead man in order to get a better look at the falcon is symbolic of his values.

Behaviorism: facial expressions

Chapter 16 provides us with eight good examples of behaviorist description: We know of the internal experience of a person only by its external manifestations. When Effie finally gets out of Sam that he knows where Brigid went, Effie's "eyes opened until their brown was surrounded by white." Her eyes even signal her internal conflict: When Sam demands that she halt her furious denunciation of his faults, "His tone brought a brief uneasy glint into her hot eyes. . . . " She is fearful she has gone too far. But then she overcomes her fear:" . . . she tossed her head and the glint vanished," and she goes further, actually threatening to notify the police if he doesn't go after Brigid.

Hammett tells much about Sam's character in a simple contrast of his facial expressions. When Sam feels inside Jacobi's coat and withdraws his hand smeared with blood, his face remains impassive. But when he unwraps Jacobi's package, his eyes are shining.

Characterization: Luke

The hotel detective both advances the action and serves as a contrast to Sam. Luke has efficiently jotted down the license number of Cairo's cab and reported that Cairo left with a suitcase. But it takes the presumably more efficient Sam to point out that Luke forgot about Cairo's trunk. That they find the trunk empty sums up Sam's success in this line of his investigation.

Characterization: Jacobi

What we've heard so far about the captain of La Paloma, and what we see in Sam's office, isn't enough to tell us whether he's an innocent victim of, or one of the participants in, the quest for the falcon. All we really know is that he is a very tenacious defender of the cargo he has delivered from Hong Kong. Apparently he managed to restore order in his cabin after one of his four guests fired a shot; did the bullet fly upward because seven-foot tall Jacobi pushed a gunhand that way? When he arrives at Sam's office, he collapses in a very significant manner: his hands protecting his package rather than reaching out to break his fall. He clutches the package as though it's the center of his existence.

Hammett's description of Jacobi-as we've treated it in several connections above-constitutes one of the most melodramatic, maybe even romantic portraits in twentieth-century literature. Suspense: Will we find out whether he was an accomplice of Brigid or simply a captain hired to get cargo to its destination? Who shot him?

Characterization: Effie

We realize in this chapter that Effie is serving four functions in the unfolding of the action and the characterization. (1) Her sympathy for Brigid keeps alive in us the belief that there must be some virtue in Brigid. (2) Effie stands for the humanitarian instincts that Spade seems to lack. If a human being has disappeared, you either do something about it yourself or you go to the police. Sam has an obligation to do the former: She is his client who hired him to protect her. (3) However, it's entirely possible that it is Effie's talking of involving the police that motivates him to get on Brigid's trail. (4) It's her anger at Sam for his slump in activity in the Brigid case that justifies her severe castigation of him. She provides strong support for all the negative things Dundy, Polhaus, and Wise have said about Sam, and all we've observed ourselves: He is spiteful, a holder of grudges, "not so damned honest," and hasn't been "so much on the level" with Brigid that she should trust him completely.

Two other aspects of Effie surface in our awareness of this chapter. (5) She is a tragic figure to the extent that she might lack an identity of her own. She identifies usually with Sam's projects or with Brigid as a person. (6) She is a tragic figure too if the critic William Nolan is right. He believes that Sam has had a sexual relationship with Effie, and that it's made obvious by her physical freedom with him: She massages him, lets him rest his head on her breast, puts her feet on his chair, and-most dramatically in this chapter-she beats his chest with her fists to drive him to pay as much attention to Brigid as to Jacobi and the falcon. Think in this connection of Brigid's hostility to Iva, and watch future developments for further clues. The tragedy, if Nolan is right, is that she has to endure his affairs with other women when she herself has been his lover.

Characterization: Spade

Of course, Effie has no more knowledge of Sam's unspoken thoughts than we do. We have to imagine why he has hesitated to search for Brigid. One possible explanation: If, as he tells Effie, he's sure Brigid went straight to La Paloma once she read the boat was in port, he has to ace these questions: Why didn't she take him with her to protect her? If the falcon is on La Paloma and she has gone there to get it, isn't she cutting him out of the deal? Instead of his selling it to Gutman for $25,000, is she going to do that herself, without the middleman Sam: To avoid giving him a share of the profits? And even when Jacobi's arrival makes it clear that somebody still wants Sam "in," it might just be another instance of what he has told Effie: Brigid includes him "in" only when she needs him. Maybe she did plan to exclude him until some new emergency forced her to send Jacobi to Sam's office.

Finally, we have in this chapter two more instances of Sam's machismo. In his joy over having the bird, he hugs her so tight he hurts her. It's as though he has always to assert his male strength. Worse, at the end he gives her the kind of praise that is insulting: "You're a damned good man, sister." In other words, women are inferior until they become masculine and then equal.

CHAPTER 17: SATURDAY NIGHT

The title is partly ironic. It tells us that on the night when most Americans are "out on the town," Sam is furiously at work. Notice too that Sam and Effie have worked all day Saturday. In 1928 most Americans worked a six-day week; in 1946 your present author, on his first civilian job, worked five-and-a half days: 44 hours, the last four on Saturday. Effie is working at least 48 hours a week: The union movement has not yet won the 40-hour week.

Function

After this chapter scatters the characters, it brings them together for the traditional end-of-the-mystery scene of the modern detective story. Usually there is just one criminal present among all the innocent suspects as the detective puts all the pieces together, explains, exonerates some people, accuses and turns the murderer over to the police. Hammett's ironic twist is that in this windup discussion, the detective is a captive of the criminals, that apparently they might even go free after they settle with him, and that we can't rely on the usual pattern to understand what will develop. For example, can we count on the police's being involved at all, as they always are in the run-of-the-mill detective story?

Diction

The cab-driver's announcement that his car is "rearing to go" is a throwback to the days when the cab was literally horse-powered and the horse, maybe chafing at the bit, might even rear up on its hind legs. The cabbie's further pronouncement that detective work is "a tough racket" is quite ironic, but probably unintentionally so. Early in the twentieth-century a racket was understood to be a shady or dishonest undertaking; by 1928 the word was used in a sarcastic way to indicate even legitimate ways of making a living. But we remember Effie's comment in the preceding chapter that Sam is "not so damned honest."

The plump man who says that "The juice is not on" in 26 Ancho is referring to the electricity. Sam's growling "I ran into a plant" is his way of saying that he was the victim of a scheme to deceive him; that is, Brigid's call to lure him to the Alexandria, and Rhea's false information that Brigid had been taken to Burlingame to be killed. The Chesterfield Effie sits on is a davenport with upright armrests at both ends.

Characterization: Rhea Gutman

Is she acting out her bizarre "drugged" condition or is it real? Her not being there when Sam returns does not necessarily mean she woke up after he left: The Gutman crew could have removed her. Surely the scratches on her hand and torso are real: Perhaps these wounds have convinced Sam she is doing all in her power to stay awake to alert him to Brigid's danger. The sensationalism of the scene includes the fact that a beautiful teenager is scarred for life for either her father's or Brigid's purposes, or both. This sacrifice makes their enterprise sound even more desperate; They must truly be after a king's ransom. Has Rhea also been intended as a sexual decoy: Why really does she greet him in pajamas and bare her torso to show the wounds? She is so beautiful she elicits from Hammett some of his best description; e.g., "her slender throat was a firm curve from chin to chest."

Characterization: Brigid

Her brief appearance-reappearance!-sums up most of the suspense until now. Has she come to be "protected" by Sam? Does she expect a renewal of their affair? Where has she been? Does she know that Sam learned about her meeting with Gutman, Cairo, Wilmer? Is she really as surprised as she seems to find that Sam has (they have?) walked into a trap?

Characterization: Spade

He seems out of control and tailspinning toward disaster. Notice that the Gutman gang have been in virtual control of his whereabouts, twice getting him out of the way when that served their purposes, and now trapping him in his own apartment when they need his presence. Since Wilmer saw Jacobi's body at Sam's office, we can assume they know he has the falcon. The more we consider his predicament, the surer we are he will have to use every trick of the trade to survive. For, after they buy the falcon from him, why should they let him live anymore than they let Archer, Thursby, and Jacobi live? And if he does live, doesn't he still have to face Bryan and Dundy about his part in the last two of those deaths?

Notice the tricks of the trade he has used in this chapter alone. He has performed a "first-aid dance" with a drugged person, gracefully moving her about the floor even while keeping an eye out for-Wilmer? Cairo? He has, it turns out, a post-office box under an assumed name (allowing him to mail the parcel check for the falcon to a place beyond Gutman's control). And he uses still another pseudonym to call the hospital about the drugged girl at the Alexandria (has he done this only on humanitarian grounds, or also so that on his return he could find out from the desk what has happened to her?). He "cases" 26 Ancho expertly: We doubt that if there were anyone inside they would be able to hear him. And notice, he doesn't talk to Effie over the phone about the Jacobi situation-he goes all the way to her house, presumably to make sure their talk is confidential.

CHAPTER 18: THE FALL GUY

Title, structure

Although Hammett's action and setting are continuous for the remainder of the novel (except for the last page), he divides that action into three chapters corresponding to the three stages in Sam's struggle against the criminals, the police, and the D.A. Chapter 18, as its title indicates, is the stage in which he wins the first round, the struggle over the need for "a fall guy."

Diction

Insisting that he and Gutman need "a fall guy," Spade means a scapegoat, a victim, Someone who would be sacrificed to save the rest of them. The phrase comes from the prevalence of crooked wrestling matches in which the two wrestlers agree in advance who will lose (take a fall).

The word "punk" as used in Sam's day was a term of contempt for a petty hoodlum, a softie who acts tough, a small-time crook, a lackey, a boy in a pederastic relationship. "Chumps," as Spade calls the police, are stupid people. By saying his "name" would be "Mud" if he doesn't produce a fall-guy, Spade means his enemies could fling mud at him, besmirch his reputation. When Wilmer tells Spade to "go for [his] heater," he's using a brand-new slang expression for draw your gun, an expression that suddenly became popular in film, fiction, and actual underworld usage about 1928. Wilmer's threat to "fog" Spade means to kill him.

Spade's being willing to "frame" Cairo or "rig" Brigid means he would send them to the gallows on the basis of false evidence. When Sam explains why they can't "bump [him] off" he means, of course, they can't kill him. And when he dubs Cairo "a pip!" he's sarcastically calling the Levantine a remarkable person.

Notice that the use of such terms gives both gangsters and policemen their own epic language to glorify themselves as men of heroic proportions.

Characterization: Gutman

By now we can characterize Gutman as an underworld figure who talks in courtly fashion, in well-rounded sentences; who prides himself on his ingratiating manner, his cajolery and sarcasm; a stylist, as are many cynics, smiling as he discusses matters like torture and murder. He rarely loses his composure and when he does, it's all the more meaningful for its rarity. Like many obese people, he has developed physical gracefulness as a result of having had to study the need and the means of moving his bulk. Also his rare resort to physical violence is astonishingly fast and effective for a fat man, as when he knocks Wilmer's gun out of his hand just as Wilmer's about to shoot the only person who knows where the falcon is spending the night.

Irony

Notice Hammett's excellent ironic foreshadowing: To get the bird Gutman has been willing to mar his daughter's beauty; this makes his protestations of wanting to treat Wilmer as his "own son" rather hollow.

Characterization: Cairo and Gutman

Notice how Hammett characterizes Cairo and Gutman partly through comparison and contrast. They are both very literate men, taking pride in their verbal style, evidence of the continuous self-control required in their "profession." We know that Gutman favors Cairo over Wilmer: Gutman listens to Cairo's whispered comments on Spade's "fall-guy" plan. But Cairo can more easily be prodded into anger than Gutman can, as when Spade knocks out Wilmer. And so Gutman is their natural leader: He can keep his head. In the fracas over Wilmer, Gutman is paternal Cairo is so childish he elicits a mock-paternalistic spanking from Spade.

Characterization: Wilmer

A major problem that Hammett faces in this scene is to depict the way a gunman, accustomed to settling things by violence, will act in a situation which things are to be settled by a long-drawn-out duel of wits. In retrospect, we can see that Spade has actually counted on Wilmer's being - in spite of his big guns - the weak link in the Gutman lineup. We can assume that the gunsel feels uneasy, at a disadvantage, when Gutman accepts Spade's refusal to be frisked. Sam's first effort to "stir things up" - his crafty remark about Rhea's "nice belly" - might have been intended to get Gutman off-balance, but - surprisingly yet credibly - it affects only Wilmer. Does he step forward gun-ready because he expects Gutman to want Sam punished for such "wolfish" talk? Callow, naive, inexperienced as Wilmer is, is he confused by this heterosexual ribaldry? When both Brigid and Cairo look at him "reproachfully," is it because they are puzzled by his unworldliness? And when he blushes, is it because he is embarrassed by his own naivete, or because he has himself some sexual interest in Rhea? It's a remarkably complex moment, one that any major author would be proud to have created.

Now Wilmer is completely off-balance, out beyond his depth, so that when Spade proposes Wilmer as their fall-guy, he acts without his boss' consent. Gutman has no choice but to disarm him, for if Wilmer killed Sam, they would have lost the falcon. Hammett's depiction of the gunsel in this critical scene is nothing short of brilliant.

Characterization: Spade

Never privy to what Sam is thinking, we can nevertheless assume, from his actions, what his strategy is: This time "stirring things up" would have to mean, again, turning the crooks one against another. As would be expected, Sam succeeds in putting both Wilmer and Cairo off balance with his long explanations of why they need a fall-guy: They are the candidates for the honor. An unexpected development, though, is that Sam subtly maneuvers Gutman into betraying an interest in the possibility of using a scapegoat. For, the longer Sam keeps Gutman on that topic, the more it must become evident even to Wilmer that Gutman is tempted by the proposal. Then, when Gutman makes his second mistake-letting the worried Cairo whisper to him-Sam has the perfect development with which to taunt Wilmer into his biggest mistake.

We've made it clear how Sam has deliberately manipulated the three male criminals. But what has motivated him? In his argument with Gutman over turning in Wilmer as a fall-guy, Spade has relied on the fact that none of them would be safe in the future unless the D.A. and the police can make at least one solid arrest to close the case. But we should see that he has other, both personal and professional reasons. He wants his revenge on the "gunsel." He has to live up to his "flyting boast" to bring in the murderer "all tied up." And Sam does seem certain that Wilmer really did the actual shooting of Thursby and Jacobi. Thus Hammett has thoroughly motivated Spade's proposal for a fall-guy, not only in personal and psychological terms, but also in legal terms: for the sake of justice.

Spade's moral ambiguity

Even though Spade has manipulated the Gutman gang to give up the actual murderer, his arguments have revealed that his ethics are deeply questionable. To get his fall guy, he apparently is agreeing to let Gutman (mastermind of the Thursby and Jacobi murders) and Cairo (at least an accomplice to the Jacobi killing) go scot free. And he probably is not joking when he says they could frame Cairo or Brigid for the murders Wilmer committed. In Hammett's short story "The Golden Horseshoe," one of his other heroes, "The Continental Op," does use false evidence to send a criminal to the gallows for a crime he didn't commit. The private eye, in other words, can appoint himself the secret judge of the criminal. Sam is not joking either, probably, when he says that-to prevent Wilmer from telling the police about the rest of them - they could arrange to have him killed resisting arrest. These are not the kinds of activities for which private eyes are licensed. Is this kind of power one of the reasons Spade enjoys his work?

Spade as Antaeus

In the course of his argument with Gutman about the need to throw a fall-guy to the police, Spade insists that he and not Gutman understands the local situation: "This is my city and my game." This comes from a cynic, a man with few pure values, and it means: "You gain strength by being rooted in to a place and a profession." In classical mythology, Antaeus was strong when he had his feet on the Earth; Hercules could defeat him only by lifting him up into the air, away from his source of strength. Spade, a man of few beliefs, is an avowed Antaean.

CHAPTER 19: THE RUSSIAN'S HAND

Title

In contrast with the intense confinement of "apartment drama," Hammett weaves his background anecdotes back and forth across time and space. Earlier we have heard of portentous events in Paris, Malta, Constantinople, Hong Kong. Now we hear from still another remote corner of the globe. In 1930 the Russian Revolution, with its emigre princes and generals, its Red and White Armies, was still an actively mysterious-to some people, exotic; to others, terrifying-drama. "The Russian's Hand," of course, adds to the effect with its ambiguity: It is both a part of the general's body and his characteristic touch.

Plot design

In his final three chapters, with their continuous action and setting, all together designed to serve as the traditional detective story wind-up, Hammett has devoted Chapter 18 to the need for a fall-guy; now he devotes Chapter 19 to the resolution of the quest for the bird. Thus he suspensefully saves Chapter 20 for the resolution of the Brigid-Sam romance.

Three features of Hammett's plotting in 19 should be especially noted. (1) When Sam has to call Effie to tell her how to get the falcon, he is surrounded by the Gutman gang. But he has so arranged things that what the gang overhears is of no use to them and can make sense only to Effie. (2) To narrate the night-long action, Hammett uses the classical Scene-Summary-Scene technique. During the hours when Sam forces Gutman to give him all the details that will hang Wilmer, and Sam "strip searches" Brigid, Hammett uses dramatization in one continuous scene (i.e., dialogue and description of action). But when they all "settle . . . down to wait the rest of the night through," Hammett uses a brief summary for the activities of each character. Then, at dawn, when it's time to call Effie, Hammett resumes the minute-by-minute dramatization.

The alternation of scene-summary-scene varies the pace and makes key events stand out over the low-key transitions. But both scenes and summaries can add to characterization and to suspense. It is significant, for example, that while waiting "the rest of the night through," Gutman can actually read, and Brigid can doze, and Wilmer-hours before his arrest for murder-can actually sleep, and Sam can be "wide-awake, cheerful, and full of vigor."

(3) Hammett's building of the climax of the falcon strain of the novel is nothing short of masterful. It deserves comparison with the crises of Sophocles' Oedipus Rex and of the Bible story of Esther. Note how Hammett makes us see and feel the rapid action by placing each character carefully in the apartment and describing each one's physical manifestations of mood.

Then note the incredibly rapid changes of mood-at least eleven distinct changes of mood and pace, all in four or so pages of print! (1) Good humor, a feeling of success, prevails as Sam and Effie joke at the door; (2) then tension grows-Gutman nears tears, Cairo rubbing his hands, Brigid chewing her lip, Sam mindful of the boy-as Gutman tears open the bundle and declares "It's it;" (3) but then swift descent into dismay as his pocket knife proves "It's a fake;" and (4) cold anger takes over as Sam demands an explanation of Brigid; (5) logical inquiry gives way to Cairo's visually-surprising, tearful dance of denunciation of Gutman's obesity and his equally fat mistakes; then (6) Gutman's amazing recovery of composure and (7) Cairo's and Gutman's laughter of relief as they agree they can easily resume their quest; (8) then we experience Sam's sour dissatisfaction as he discovers the boy has escaped; (9) we experience still another surprise as Gutman-for the first time-becomes his own gunman, robbing Sam at gunpoint of the money paid for delivery of the bird; (10) and still another kind of shock - the shock of recognition of how opposites meet - as Gutman invites Sam to join them in their eighteenth year of the quest; (11) finally a kind of numb exhaustion takes over as we realize the jeopardy Sam is in: With no fall-guy he is himself now wide open to Dundy's and the D.A.'s charges and to the threat posed by Wilmer's being out there.

Diction

In telling Effie how to get the "bird" from the parcel room, Sam uses the abbreviation "p.d.q." instead of the real curse words, pretty damned quickly. Note too that this time Sam, in saying ". . . he's not a fall-guy unless he's a cinch to take the fall," pegs the term fall-guy on its original wrestling use: the wrestler who agrees to lose. And to prove again he's cultivated, Gutman tells Sam he's leaving him the rara avis as a memento. That's Latin for rare bird.

Ironies

Chapter 19 explodes and glows with ironies big and small. There are two major reversals of expectation. The falcon, to which they have devoted so much ingenuity, conspiracy, and time, proves to be a fake. The fall-guy, supposed to be Sam's salvation, escapes. As the plot rises to those dramatic anti-climaxes, the characters reveal their tensions in their frequent resort to sarcasm.

Characterization: Cairo

In spite of his blubbering and sulking, in spite of Wilmer's rejection of him, Cairo recovers some stature in this chapter. Since it was he who had the intelligence to see the connections between La Paloma's arrival and Brigid's being in Frisco, we understand now how he gained his way back into Gutman's graces. And since he now begs Gutman not to give Sam a fall-guy, we must infer that his whispering earlier with Gutman was not what Sam had made of it (a sellout of Wilmer). By chapter's end we have recovered sufficient respect for his intelligence to give credence to his explanation for why they got a fake falcon from Kemidov: Gutman had tipped his hand by letting the general know how valuable the bird is. And surely we're not surprised when Cairo giggles and decides to join Gutman in his renewed search for the bird - and when Gutman accepts-because they seem, ironically, to be more interested in the hunt itself than in its results.

Characterization: Brigid

To appreciate Gutman's revelations about her activities, we have to imagine how they are affecting Sam. Gutman says Thursby was fully loyal to Brigid, which doubtless tells Sam that she lied to him about Thursby too. Gutman's telling Sam that he had "persuaded" her to work with him probably makes Sam distrustful of her role in the final evening: for example, her confiding that he was "killing something" when he insisted on searching her. We must remember too what Sam must have felt when he realized that she had put the $10,000 in her pocket: Would she have tried to escape with it, if Gutman hadn't demanded to know where it was? Perhaps the most damning moment of all is a slip-of-the tongue she makes that nobody comments on - but will Sam keep it in mind as he totes up the evening? When Sam suspects that she is the one who substituted a fake bird for the real one, she cries out: "No, ... that is the one I got from Kemidov, I swear - " Doesn't that sound as if she has known all along there are other birds?

Our overall impression of Brigid as described by Gutman-a formidable woman in control of her situation and difficult to deal with-quite contradicts the role she has played for Sam-that of the helpless one in need of protection.

Characterization: Wilmer

If we could be inside "the gunsel's" mind, we might discover that maybe worse for him than Spade's overpowering him is Gutman's abandonment of him. He has, after all, been Gutman's faithful lackey. He has risked his life for Gutman. And now, when Gutman is vicious in his sarcasm (" ... if you lose a son, it's possible to get another - and there's only one Maltese falcon"), Hammett pictures the "son" as just sitting there "keeping his cold hazel eyes on Gutman's face." Hammett follows this ghastly image with one of Wilmer "breathing heavily" at the sight of the bird for which he has murdered two men. Then, when Sam realizes that Wilmer has escaped, "the boy" resumes his sinister, suspenseful role as the threat outside the "apartment drama."

Characterization: Gutman

This is another part of Hammett's irony: Whereas in the traditional detective story it's the private eye who puts all the pieces together, in the case of the Maltese falcon it's the master criminal (Gutman) who is forced by circumstances to make sense of it all. Gutman's judgments of Brigid and Cairo make such good sense that we believe too his estimate for a character we have never had a chance to judge for ourselves: Thursby. Gutman impresses us too with the truth of his estimate of Sam as a man who would make a good criminal, a valuable partner in the next Gutman-Cairo enterprise.

Characterization: Spade

In addition to what we've already observed in his interaction with others (above), we should comment on Spade's positivism, cynicism, and ethics as revealed in this the penultimate chapter.

Positivism. Sam's strip-search of Brigid is a perfect example of his scientific skepticism or positivism. She protests that she does not have the missing $1,000 bill and that, because of their love, he should believe her. He insists there is only one way for him to be sure. After the search proves she was (for once) telling the truth, he says simply, "Now I know." Only first-hand, empirical evidence, verifiable facts, count. But this fact-finding does allow him to reason to a second conclusion: If Brigid hasn't palmed the bill, and the only other person to have handled the bills is Gutman, then Gutman palmed it. In Gutman's case, then, the strip-search is not necessary. This is scientific positivism at work and is one reason detective-fiction is sometimes considered a branch of science fiction.

Cynicism. When Cairo's solicitude annoys the "gunsel" and the latter strikes the former, Spade alludes to Shakespeare when he remarks to Brigid: "The course of true love. ... " The rest of Shakespeare's line is " ... never did run smooth." This is first of all another of his sneering remarks about homosexual passion (which, ironically, was common in Shakespeare's day as now). Secondly, he clearly wants Brigid to see what he thinks of "love" generally, including theirs, which he will discuss further in the final chapter. This is his skepticism carried to the point of cynicism: the denial of any subjective values.

Ethics. Sam says to Gutman, when demanding facts he can use to prosecute Wilmer, "You're staying out of jail and ... getting the falcon." This seems to be a compromise, a bargain that nets the law the actual hired killer of Thursby and Jacobi in exchange for letting the killer's boss go free. If the falcon proved to be real, would Spade carry out the bargain? Now that the falcon proves to be fake, need he? Will he? In any event, this is certainly not clear-cut ethics, but ethics up for bargaining.

One way of characterizing Spade's ethics is to keep in mind that throughout his dealings with the underworld, Spade has been so close to their methods, their attitudes, that Gutman admires him and offers him a partnership in their ongoing Maltese falcon enterprise.

Theme

Gutman has spent seventeen years in his quest for the falcon. Sam has spent an intense four-day period for it, has risked his life, freedom, and reputation for it. And now it proves to be "a fake." The quest for a false falcon has become an allegory for humanity's vain greed for material wealth, for humanity's willingness to suspend all sense of ethics while in the pursuit of riches.

THE MALTESE FALCON

TEXTUAL ANALYSIS

CHAPTER 20

CHAPTER 20: IF THEY HANG YOU

Title

Hammett picked for his title the phrase with the greatest poignance and the most suspense for the reader coming upon it for the first time. In retrospect, though, these sentences take on a note of bitterest satire about the values of romantic love.

Function: Plot Resolution

As we have noted earlier, Hammett devotes his last three chapters to the solution of mysteries that both the detective-story tradition and the logic of his own novel require. Traditionally, at the end the detective convenes all the people involved, explains everything, puts all the pieces together, presents the evidence against the guilty one, and exonerates and releases the others.

Spade's problem has been different. The people he is meeting are all guilty. He has entered the final scene (Chapters 18, 19, 20) with incomplete evidence, and he has had to turn the criminals against each other (18), get them to fill in the details he still lacks, and then let them leave (19), except one with whom he has to deal separately (20). When we finish the novel, we can look back and realize that Spade could have handled the conclusion no other way. In other words, the very order in which he commands events is evidence of his mastery of the criminal mind.

Sam's staging of events in this way provides us too, of course, with a spacing out of the climaxes of the four separate strains of the plot: the isolation of the murderer of Thursby and Jacobi (18), the resolution of the mystery of the Maltese falcon (19), and now the double resolution of the case of the murder of Archer and of the romantic affair between Sam and Brigid (20).

Diction

As befits the main character in hardboiled fiction, Spade uses another burst of slang expressions in his wind-up talks with Brigid. Saying to Brigid, "I'm in this with you and you're not going to gum it," Sam means she's not going to ruin or spoil the situation. Today he'd be more likely to say gum it up, or gum up the works. The figure of speech derives from the practice, by saboteurs, of placing a gummy substance into a mechanism to prevent its moving parts from working well. Telling Brigid, "I'm going to send you over," Sam means he's going to send her to prison. In other parts of the country, or at other times, Sam might say send you up. The main thrust of Sam's message is summed up in his statement, "I won't play the sap for you," that is I'm no fool, you can't take advantage of me.

Metaphor

Spade uses two metaphors to pressure Brigid into telling him the truth fast: "We're sitting on dynamite...." and "The pair of us sitting under the gallows." Neither situation is literally true, and even if the second might materialize, the first remains a rhetorical comparison by which Sam explains to Brigid the danger they are in by likening it to a situation that is explosive and fatal. Notice that Sam says not you but we, us: He is using as an extra inducement the notion that he is with her in this crisis. As soon as he gets out of her the details he needs, he changes the pronoun, saying, in effect, "You are sitting on dynamite," and saying, in actuality, "If they hang you...."

Characterization: Spade

The typical detective story culminates in the triumph of logic over crime, as an expert sleuth, through investigation, observation, and deduction, finally identifies the criminal. Usually the detective is working against forces outside himself. But *The Maltese Falcon* culminates in a double triumph for rationalism. Spade uses logic not only to identify the murderer of Miles Archer but also to quell irresponsible forces inside himself.

That Spade endures internal as well as external conflict is one of the reasons that Falcon is rated above its genre, as genuine literature. And because the point of view Hammett uses denies the reader access to Spade's thinking until he himself reveals it in speech, we have not learned the real nature of his conflict until this the final chapter. And this of course has intensified the suspense because until Chapter 20 Hammett has represented Spade's internal commotion only behavioristically-

that is, through its manifestations in Spade's physical, non-verbal behavior.

We have not until now known, then, that apparently Spade realized, almost immediately after seeing Archer's body, that Brigid was his killer. Now we can understand what he was thinking about, in Chapter 2, when he sat on his bed for nearly an hour, drinking rum and rolling and smoking cigarettes. And maybe we know too now why he muttered "Damn her" when the street doorbell rang and he thought it was a woman-Brigid? By then he must have reasoned through to the only explanation that would ever make sense: That no one could have lured Miles into a blind alley and got so close to him without his drawing a gun-except his client on that job, Brigid.

Sam's motivation

Our next concern then is one of motivation: Why has Spade taken so many chances in concealing his knowledge (of Archer's killer) from both the police and Brigid? For four days he has been in great peril as an accomplice after the fact; and how could he be sure Brigid would not shoot other people, maybe him?

We can assume only two reasons for his keeping the secret of Archer's death. First, Spade's own sexual interest in Brigid. There could be no long-range relation with her (as he now makes clear): He could never feel safe with her. But he could play it out, for both personal and professional reasons, for as long as it could last. This ties in with a second reason: In that hour of thinking on the bed, he must have figured that to arrest her then would cut short an investigation that should go beyond her. She and Thursby must have seemed to him to be part of a larger group of people involved. And when Dundy and Polhaus brought the news that now Thursby too had been killed, this must have confirmed Sam's suspicions. And they have since been authenticated.

If Sam had accused and arrested Brigid right after he figured out she had killed Miles (Chapter 2), neither the police nor Spade might ever have learned of the existence of Gutman, Cairo, Wilmer, Jacobi. Indeed, with Cairo's deduction about La Paloma's arrival, Gutman might have got the falcon directly. With Thursby dead and Brigid under arrest, what would have stopped Gutman from getting the bird himself?

So Sam's policy of waiting for them to come to him, continuing to play along with Brigid, and stirring things up, while it was a great risk, has paid off.

Just as masterful as his use of logic to solve the murders and arrest the survivors is his use of reason to quell his own personal passion. Maybe he does love Brigid but, as he has been cautious enough to note, she has used sex to control Thursby, Archer, Jacobi and maybe even the Russian general (we can infer that from what she says about him in Chapter 9). She has counted on Sam's also "playing the sap," and even Gutman has counted on Sam's being one more "sucker" on her list.

Sam's quelling his own passion for Brigid is not all logic, we should note. It's part cynicism too. He seems to feel that a sexual attachment wouldn't last more than a month in any event.

Perhaps we should even say that Sam's turning Brigid over to the police is not all logic either. It's largely a matter of devotion to a code; sometimes blind devotion. A detective is devoted to detecting, to protecting other detectives, and to the prestige of the profession. Spade is more devoted to that code than to the letter of the law. He will, if necessary, break the law to live blindly by the code. Logic is his means of living up to the code.

Like Chapter 3, Chapter 20 could also be titled "Three Women." Sam gives up Brigid for the sake of the code and his own neck. He loses-for the time being at least- the affection of Effie because he has put logic and the code above romance. And in the last line he shivers when Iva enters because, as we well know by now, that is a cold, cold relationship; that is not romance. For Sam, as for many American males, his job is his passion.

Characterization: Brigid

She has made two mistakes with Sam. She has underestimated his detective skills. It has not occurred to her that he has already identified her as Archer's killer and has watched her with that knowledge for four days now. And she has underestimated his ability to resist her sexual charms.

But what motivates her? How did she get to be this way? Is it enough to say, as many critics do, that she has learned that her sexual beauty gives her power and she uses it to get what she wants? That she is a literary type, a femme fatale, a siren, a succubus, an irresistible woman who leads men into danger and disaster?

Surely she is all that, but in Chapter 20 we can also pick up some clues to her individual psychological history. Sam and Brigid talk of her need for help and protection. On a mission for Gutman, she asked Cairo for help in getting the falcon for herself. Then, distrusting Cairo, she sought Thursby's help, but distrusting Thursby, sought Spade's help, etc. This pattern of seeking help and then fearing the helper suggests that she had a father who failed to protect her as she thought she needed protection, toward whom she felt ambivalent as a consequence, now trusting, now distrusting him. Perhaps Gutman became a father figure, then she distrusted him and sought Cairo's help, and has kept going around in this cycle until Sam has broken it.

Sam felt as early as Chapter 6 that hers is a life of such routines and he could get caught up in them. He told her then that her speech, about how bad she was, was "a speech you've practiced." And notice how she again bears out his observation in Chapter 20. She uses on Sam the same cliche speech that must have worked on count less men: "I would have come back to you.... From the first instant I saw you I knew - "

We should note too that Hammett's idea of a femme fatale, a siren, is a macho idea, the same notion that since Eve in the Garden, Helen of Troy, and Delilah in Gaza, all of man's troubles could and should be blamed on women.

Characterization: Polhaus

"Get them?" asks Sam. "Got them," replies Polhaus. And in this laconic dialogue we see that Tom knows, at last, that Spade does appreciate and respect him. Indeed, Sam has more than made it up to Tom. The sergeant gets the glory of the capture, now he gets the "exhibits" too, and one more unexpected prisoner to boot. Perhaps best of all, Tom's trust in Sam has been justified. But we can also tell, from Sam's manic behavior in the presence of the silent-accuser Dundy, that Tom's work as mediator is not a thing of the past.

Characterization: Effie

What does she mean by "that" when she asks Sam "You did that . . . to her?" Does she think that Sam has dispassionately used sex to help solve a crime? Or does she feel that there was love between him and Brigid, and Sam should have put love above the law? If it's the latter, she's Hammett's further evidence that the conflict between the code and romance is not easily resolved. Indeed, when Sam's face turns "pale as his collar" perhaps it's partly because Effie has reminded him of the conflict. In any event, Effie expresses what should be added to the story: There is something awesome about a man who can sleep with a woman one day and arrest her the next; that is, rise above the subjective and obey the objective requirement.

We must keep in mind that Effie has so identified with Brigid (as Sam's "beloved"? of his "victim"?) that Effie feels she herself has been betrayed. Her romantic side is in a chaotic state of mind; but her logical side knows he'r "right." She too will yield, as Sam has, to the demands of objectivity.

Theme

The meaning of the conclusion is that logic can and must prevail over crime in the social sphere, and over irresponsible passion in the personal sphere.

THE MALTESE FALCON

CHARACTER ANALYSES

Using the eight methods of characterization we have identified, Hammett creates in *The Maltese Falcon* at least twenty memorable and unique characters. Now we offer, in alphabetical order, critical analyses of these characterizations. For a more detailed study, you should check the relevant Characterization sections in our "Textual Analyses." Our references to those sections will also remind you of the exact chapters in the Falcon in which each character appears.

Archer, Iva

She is so wrong about Sam's true feelings toward her that she actually thinks he killed her husband so he could marry her. Her marriage with Archer is now revealed to have been a spiteful, bitter, neurotic relationship with a womanizing Miles, who refused to grant her a divorce. Iva herself is mean, petty, sentimental and manipulative, given to staging jealous tricks like sending the police to Sam's apartment when she knows Brigid is there. Iva's arrival in his office the morning after he has sent Brigid to jail is intended to emphasize his failure to find real romance, his loneliness in such a cold relationship. (See also Characterization: Iva in "Textual Analysis" of Hammett's Chapters 3 and 11.)

Archer, Miles

Hammett shrewdly gives him a mock-heroic tag-name. His first name is Latin for soldier, a good tag for a man who carries a gun. His last name is the English name for the constellation Sagittarius. In astrology, the Archer is pictured as (1) a centaur, half-beast (horse) and half-man, and is regarded as (2) both the arrow (the hunter) and the target (the hunted). So his name is ironically apt: (1) Acting toward the new client like a slobbering, lecherous animal, he is lured to his death precisely because he is, as Spade puts it, "a sucker over women." (2) Hired to track Thursby, he winds up himself the victim. As a husband, he was, on the one hand, a man who taunted his wife with his opportunities with other women, and was, on the other hand, a cuckold, unaware his wife was sleeping with his partner. Sam describes him as "a louse," whom Sam planned to throw out of the firm when their contract year was up. (See also Characterization: Archer in "Textual Analysis" of Hammett's Chapter 1.)

Bryan, District Attorney

He's right, if he could know who Sam's client is-that is, "who Archer was shadowing Thursby for" - Bryan would know more about the whole case. We know (dramatic irony) that if he could interrogate Brigid, he might clear up the question of who killed Thursby. He's right, Spade might very well be an accomplice after the fact. But Bryan is wrong in his tactics. It isn't true that a man who's unwilling to make "guesses" in front of the D.A. must therefore have something to conceal. It isn't true that a man who invokes the Fifth Amendment thereby shows he's guilty. As the D.A. should be the first one to declare and affirm, the Fifth Amendment was included in the Bill of Rights so that the authorities can't use confessions extracted under torture or intimidation, or from a suspect who has been forced to talk without having legal counsel to advise him of the consequences of what he says.

Hammett's point here seems to be: Just as Spade is right in his ends but wrong in his means, so are the authorities. And it's more serious when the authorities act as if the ends justify the means because they are supposed to be models for the rest of us: The authorities are supposed to be NOT above the law.

Hammett makes District Attorney Bryan, at 45 still blond and with the jaw of an orator, memorable as a bully who relies on threats and innuendos to get his work done. (See also Characterization: Bryan in our "Textual Analysis" of Hammett's Chapter 15.)

Cairo, Joel

He is in part a literary type, in part a Hammett "original." A common figure in modern literature is "the Levantine," A man who is derived from both European and Near Eastern stocks and is therefore able to serve as a middleman between the two cultures. Hammett identifies Cairo in that tradition by tagging him with the name Cairo (major city in the Eastern Mediterranean area), by having him wear chypre, a perfume produced in the Eastern Mediterranean island of Cyprus, and by referring to him outright as "the Levantine." (Chypre is French for Cyprus; Levant is French for rising: The Near East is the area, for Europeans at least, where the sun rises.)

Hammett further distinguishes Cairo as a homosexual, and to some extent with the unfortunate misunderstanding of that sexual choice common in 1928 even to medical and psychiatric authorities. Cairo's being gay functions in three ways in the plot: it provides the reason why Brigid can taunt and provoke Cairo to anger; it provides the basis for Cairo's sympathy for Wilmer when "the boy" is being considered as the fall-guy Spade demands; and it gives Spade one more way to show how macho he is: he can ridicule a "queer," as Effie calls Cairo.

Cairo has other functions in the novel. He gives Sam information that allows him to realize that a black-bird statuette is what Brigid is also after. Cairo also helps characterize Spade as someone who'd prefer making money to making arrests: Cairo says, in effect, that that's Spade's reputation. Cairo is also one of the characters who make it clear that there's an affinity between the criminal mind and the detective mind, that they breathe the same air, use the same jargon, and think along the same lines. This compatibility is demonstrated, in Cairo's case, when, just hours after he and Spade have engaged in savage physical combat, they can meet calmly and resume their relationship.

Cairo is developed as a shrewd antagonist. He comes to Spade because he senses there's a connection between the seemingly separate killings of Thursby and of Spade's partner Archer. It is Cairo who sees in the arrival of La Paloma a connection to the presence of Brigid. He picks up quickly on Spade's tall story to the police and acts out his part perfectly, even when he is "grilled" separately by the "bulls." And it is Cairo who figures out how Gutman actually helped Kemidov deceive the Gutman gang.

Cairo is as much devoted to style in language as to style in dress. He takes pride in expressing himself in ironic, well-turned sentences. His careful attention to good speech is symbolic of the careful control of his behavior that a man of his "calling" must exert. His pride in suavity is indicated in his ability, in the midst of such a dangerous enterprise, to attend a Shakespeare play.

Like Gutman, Cairo proves at the end to be perhaps as much interested in the hunt for the prize as in the prize itself. It's a great dramatic moment for Hammett when he sees the value of having Cairo giggle as he takes off-so he thinks-to the Levant once more. (See also Characterization: Cairo in our "Textual Analysis" of Hammett's Chapters 4, 5, 7, 8, 10, 18, 19.)

Caretaker

He exemplifies Hammett's ability to bring to life every single character, no matter how "unimportant." Even though the caretaker of 26 Ancho figures in only a few pages of action, Hammett distinguishes him with a quick sequence of very human reactions. Interrupted in his enjoyment of his evening newspaper, he hesitates to admit Spade into the mysterious house. But when Sam produces his private eye ID, the caretaker's attitude changes, as though he feels this will be manly adventure, better than the paper. But after he leads Sam and his chauffeur to the house-door, he gives Sam the key and then lags behind-safe.

Chauffeur

He's another clear demonstration of Hammett's ability to breathe life into everyone who figures in the action, no matter how briefly. We know before he arrives that he's considered trustworthy because Sam asked for such a chauffeur. He proves to be cheery and something of a wit, cooperative and more courageous than the caretaker.

Cook, Wilmer

In the history of detective fiction, he is famous as the original "gunsel." This is Hammett's clever pun combining the meanings of gunman and gunsel, the latter word originally denoting a boy used for pederastic purposes by an older man. Hammett makes the boy a revolting figure, sickly white, sneering, unable to look anybody in the eyes, usually lurking on the distant edge of one's awareness, unable to talk except in cheap tough-guy phrases. We suggest early on that his manner, and his big guns, are his way of compensating for his short stature. Hammett said that Wilmer was modeled on a thief who glorified in the name the press gave him: "The Midget Bandit."

Surely he is a persistent "shadow" and an excellent shot, as we see when we learn it was Wilmer who had put four handgun bullets into Thursby from the other side of broad Geary Street.

For all Wilmer's toughness and his big "heaters," Spade correctly surmises that this "punk" is the weak link in the G-chain. Wilmer is used to settling disputes with guns and he's off-balance in a duel of wits. It takes just three phrases for Spade to drive "the boy" berserk: "nice belly," "fall-guy," and "selling you out." (See also Characterization: Wilmer-or The Youth, The Boy, The Undersized Shadow-in our "Textual Analysis" of Hammett's Chapters 10, 13, 18, 19.)

Dundy, Lieutenant

He starts out as a type: the professional police detective who (1) resents the privileges given to private detectives. But Hammett increases and individualizes the reasons Dundy has for resenting Spade. Dundy (2) has long suspected that Spade abuses his privileges and has long expected, any case now, to catch Sam at something illegal. In the Archer-Thursby cases Dundy (3) is actually handicapped in his official investigation because Spade will not divulge the name of his client who hired Archer to trail Thursby. When Dundy also (4) discovers legitimate reasons to suspect that Sam has played a direct role in the killings, the hostility between the two reaches a point at which Dundy is actually tormented into hitting Spade-a grievous mistake that puts a man in the right in the wrong! Even at novel's end, when Spade has delivered the criminals to the police, Dundy maintains a sulky silence in Sam's presence. We are left with the uncomfortable feeling that their nasty rivalry will survive this case. Dundy is a decent, conscientious, uncorruptible police officer who just has the bad luck to work in the same town as Sam Spade.

Flitcraft, Charles (Pierce)

He is one of several characters we only hear about. In one of two instances in the novel of a "story within a story" Spade tells Brigid about one of his most intriguing cases. Flitcraft was a perfectly normal business and family man who one day, on his way to lunch, was nearly hit by a beam that fell from eight or ten stories up in a construction job. Flitcraft was appalled that his life-which he conducted in a sane, logical, and well-organized manner-could have been crushed without warning by a chance event. At lunch he reasoned it out: If Nature and reality are governed by chaos and chance, then he would live his life that way.

Without warning to business associates or family, he disappeared, wandering aimlessly for years. Finally, he settled down again, into a marriage and a business quite like his earlier circumstances, but under the name of Charles Pierce.

In this characterization Hammett makes use of two tagnames. Flitcraft is the name of a man who proves to be good at the craft of flitting; indeed, in some areas of the English-speaking world, to flit can mean to move (one's residence).

Then, when Flitcraft gives himself a new name-Charles Pierce-Hammett is combining a new tag-name with a literary allusion. For Charles Sanders Pierce (1838-1914) was a great American philosopher who wrote *Chance, Love, and Logic* (which appeared posthumously in 1923, five years before Hammett wrote *Falcon*).

The detailed ways in which Peircean philosophy dovetails into *The Maltese Falcon* are explored at length in our "Textual Analysis" of Hammett's Chapter 7.

The message that Spade seems to infer from his experience in contacting Pierce-his former wife, Mrs. Flitcraft, was Spade's client-is this; True, Nature and reality may seem to be haphazard. But man is a rational animal by nature, and he survives by creating, and living by, as much order in his area of reality as he possibly can. The relevance to Spade's own profession is clear: Out of the mystery surrounding a crime, the private eye finds the rational explanation.

Flitcraft, incidentally, is a reincarnation of a character named Ashcraft in Hammett's short story "The Golden Horseshoe," one of three of his earlier stories related in theme and situation to the *The Maltese Falcon*.

Gutman, Mr. ("G")

The tag-name that Hammett gives to the leader of the criminals draws literal attention to his "gut" (or expansive waist) and ironic attention to his morality ("Gut" means good in German). Hammett's metaphor for how Gutman looks (like a mass of "bulbs" that jostle for position as he moves about) is one of the author's two great feats of description in this novel (the other being his detailed attention to changes in the characters' facial expressions). Gutman's mastery of how to maneuver his great bulk around-which he does with smoothness-connotes control of people and situations beyond himself. He is indeed the author of the situation to which every other character must address her/him self: Note that even if Brigid and Cairo have tried to take the project away from him, they are forced to return to his camp. He can order the killing of Thursby merely as a message to Brigid. He is author not only of the overall strategy of the pursuit of the bird but also of all the tactics that must be improvised: the drugging of Spade, the use of Rhea and Brigid to get Spade out of the way, the ambush in Spade's own home. When forced to adapt, Gutman can accept a plan by another author, as he accepts Spade's "fall-guy" notion.

Gutman loves language as much as Cairo does; the two of them strive for control of language almost as evidence of how they must exert detailed control to survive in their world. But Cairo is usually graceful in his speech, while Gutman tends toward the ponderous, as though a fat man is expected to use fat language. In overall control and composure, however, Gutman is the superior of Cairo. The Levantine can lose his composure when things go wrong, can indeed blubber in a tantrum, but Gutman can take any setback in his stride. It is Gutman who realizes that if the statuette they have fought for is a fake, then they need only go back to the Levant and seek out the real one. He so completely regains his composure that it proves to be his tragic flaw: He forgets that Wilmer is out there somewhere, doubtless in a vengeful mood. (See also Characterization: Gutman in our "Textual Analysis" of Hammett's Chapters 11, 131, 18, 19.)

Gutman, Rhea

Family relations in Falcon don't speak well for that institution. The Archers are hateful to each other, spiteful, neurotic, and childless. Effie seems headed toward spinsterhood or at least a non-family future. Sam mentioned one relative, his mother, and only as part of an impersonal joke. He sees love as lasting maybe a month. Though Brigid protests her "love," she never speaks of marriage or maternity. Gutman tosses the boy he regards as his son to the police as a "fall-guy," and "the fat man" sacrifices his daughter's beauty to get Sam out of the way for a few hours.

We may be in doubt about whether Rhea is so badly "drugged" as she affects, but there's no doubt that the steel-pin scratches on her torso are bloody real. They served his purpose, Gutman says. And they served the needs of the plot too, letting us see how grim and desperate Gutman is, how great the prize he seeks.

Has Rhea cooperated willingly with her father, or have they inflicted all that on her because she is his daughter to dispose of as he wants? Was she able to leave by herself after Sam took off for Burlingame, or was the gang nearby to spirit her away before the ambulance arrived? Why was Wilmer so upset at Sam's remark about her "nice belly"? All we can infer for sure about her at the end is that she is now a scarred orphan. (See also Characterization: Rhea Gutman in our "Textual Analysis" of Hammett's Chapter 17.)

Jacobi, Captain

He is a character we only hear about until the last few moments of his life, when he suddenly staggers mortally wounded into Sam's office, the falcon in his hands. Whether he is one of the real criminals is doubtful; he seems to be another of Brigid's dupes. He is certainly a powerful man albeit doomed. So tall he looks tubular, he quells a dispute in his cabin after only one shot is fired; and even after his chest is all shot out by Wilmer, Jacobi still manages to run with his parcel from Brigid's hotel to Sam's office before he expires. (See also Characterization: Jacobi in our "Textual Analysis" of Hammett's Chapter 17.)

Kemidov, General

A mysterious figure that we only hear about (from Brigid, Gutman, and Cairo). Apparently he owned a real Maltese falcon statuette but substituted for it the fake one that Brigid and Cairo have acquired. Cairo blames Gutman for this because "G", he says, gave Kemidov too much information about the bird's real value. Living in Constantinople in the Twenties, General Kemidov might be an emigre, a refugee from the Russian Revolution, during which he might have served in the White (Tsarist) Army.

Luke

There are three kinds of detectives in the Falcon: police detectives like Polhaus, independent private detectives like Sam, and hotel detectives like Luke. The last serves several functions in the story and the characterization: He alerts Sam to Cairo's movements; he too gives us the opinion that Sam is "a tough one to figure out;" he slips up once and thus shows us that Sam, who catches the slip, is the better sleuth. (See also Characterization:Luke in our "Textual Analysis" of Hammett's Chapter 16.)

O'Shaughnessy, Brigid (a.k.a. Ms. Wonderly or Ms. Leblanc)

She lives out one monstrous lie after another, rehearses and acts out whatever role suits her purpose of the moment: Often, e.g., it's the frightened, shy girl in need of a strong protector. She has the power to engage the profound sympathy of other (e.g., Effie) but usually uses it, in conjunction with her sexual powers, to enslave men in her schemes.

Her first fatal error is to assume that Sam has not identified her as Archer's killer, that Sam believes her story that Thursby was the murderer. She acts for four days unaware that Sam knows the truth.

Her second fatal error is to assume, after her success with Kemidov, Thursby, Jacobi, and Archer, that she has also enslaved Sam. His tactic has been to accept her sexual favors while maintaining his objectivity.

A woman who dupes others as a way of life, Brigid is now unwittingly used by Sam to help him identify the other criminals involved.

Her tag-name is an ironic pun. Brigid was an Irish goddess of fertility and wisdom, identified later with the Christian Saint Brigid (Bridget). To make sure we see this relationship, Hammett gives his Brigid an Irish surname. In English, her given name also sounds like Bridge-it, which is her unintended service to Sam: She serves as his bridge to the rest of the criminals.

(See also the characterizations above of others who have interacted with Brigid, and Characterization: Brigid (or Ms. Wonderly, or Ms. Leblanc) in our "Textual Analysis" of Hammett's Chapters 1, 4, 6, 7, 8, 9, 10, 17, 19, 20.)

Perine, Effie

In his characterization of Sam's assistant, Hammett depicts the development of a personality conflict that is widened and unresolved at novel's end. For, when tensions are resolved into a successful conclusion for Sam Spade and Tom Polhaus, they are only intensified for Effie.

At the beginning, she is portrayed mainly as a loyal supporter of her boss, his "girl Friday," whose last name is significant: A perine is the outer cover that protects a grain of pollen; Ms. Perine works in the outer office largely to protect her boss by screening his visitors and his callers, and even by concealing certain situations from the police. She is uncomplaining when her work exposes her to unpredictable hours and even to mortal danger. She is depicted too as a candid and very caring critic of her employer, reminding him at crucial moments that he can be "too slick" for his own good and is not always "so honest" as he should be. At one crisis, Effie exerts her power to coerce Sam into action when he hesitates to check on the whereabouts and safety of Brigid.

It's Brigid who plunges Effie into her tragic state. For Effie is a romantic and so identifies with the beautiful Brigid that she is shocked when her boss jails Brigid for murder. Is Effie shocked because she thinks Sam cold-bloodedly used sex to help solve the case? Or because she thinks he put the law above love?

Effie-whose first name is uncomfortably close to "iffy" and "effort" - is described by Hammett as somewhat of a tomboy in appearance. This could make her feel inferior in the presence of the voluptuous Brigid and the beautiful Iva. Effie is praised by Sam as "a damned good man, sister." This assessment, suggesting that a woman is inferior until she acts manlike, would be called insulting today. Some critics see her frantic remarks at the end ("Don't touch me-not now,") as revealing that she has had a sexual relationship too with Sam, which would further deepen the tragedy of her involvement with him. (For more details, see Characterization: Effie in "Textual Analysis" of Hammett's Chapters 1, 3, 4, 14, 16, 20.)

Polhaus, Thomas

Although Polhaus is a minor character, Hammett is able to skillfully represent him as going through inner as well as outer conflict. As a police detective sergeant, he is continually caught in the crossfire between his boss, Lieutenant Dundy, and his friend, the private eye Sam Spade. Polhaus apparently defends

Spade to Dundy as much as he tries to explain Dundy to Sam. Tom understands Dundy's distrust of Spade's ethics and often steps between them to lower the temperature. And Tom understands Spade's resentment of Dundy's dislike. Unfortunately Tom's defending Spade, and Tom's helping Spade in every way he can, does not earn Tom the private eye's appreciation. Of a grudging and paranoid nature, Spade tends to lump all the police together as his enemies. Tom smarts under this ingratitude and clearly wishes Sam would return his respect and affection. Tom gives Sam practical, factual help as well as psychological support, e.g., Tom gives Sam background information about Thursby that proves helpful to Spade when he's under pressure at the D. A.'s, and when he "settles" accounts with Brigid.

So we're relieved when, at the end, Tom is rewarded magnificently. It is Tom-not Dundy, not the D.A.-to whom Spade turns over the Gutman gang, Brigid, and the hard-won exhibits that will help convict them. This is a whole spectrum of feathers in Tom's cap. In addition to his getting the credit for the arrests, Tom will probably now stand vindicated in the police department for his confidence in Spade. Hammett achieves this complex relationship, with its many nuances, entirely through moody dialogue. (For more details, see Characterization: Polhaus or/and Dundy in "Textual Analysis" of Hammett's Chapters 2 and 20.)

Spade, Samuel

He is the first great example, in the genre of detective fiction, of the "hardboiled" private detective. He is a hard drinker, a chain smoker, a master of macho techniques, from rolling a cigarette to losing a "tail," to disarming a man (behind or alongside him). He is tough in his language, therefore seems to be candid, but in reality is quite selective in what he reveals. His every word, his every step, is deliberate, and even his facial expressions can be intentional. He might, for example, feign boredom and indifference while listening and watching for clues. The only time we see ecstasy in his face is when he is about to knock a man out (Cairo, Wilmer).

He maintains a furious pace while working on a case. In the Archer-Thursby case he has an extra incentive to drive fast toward a solution: To get all the information he needs, he has to let Brigid stay free; this is a terrible risk he's taking because he thus becomes an accomplice after the fact, and because she could kill again and/or escape at any time.

A loner, he rides rough-shod over other people's sentiments and feelings. Luke, Wise, Polhaus all agree that he is severe in his relations with others. "Don't overdo it," he tells Brigid when she praises him.

He never gives us a clue to what he's thinking or has just discovered. He controls his own emotions when he has to, as when Dundy hits him, but he obeys Newton's Law (every action produces a reaction) afterwards, giving furious and obscene vent to his feelings.

He arrogates to himself the right to bend the law. For example, it is against the law to lie to the police. Spade does it as a matter of course. He obviously believes that his ends justify his ignoble means. He hates the district attorney for arrogating to himself exactly those same rights.

From his Flitcraft Parable and his statements to Wise, Bryan, and Brigid, and from the way he acts, we can infer a very definite Sam Spade philosophy:

He can't believe or trust anybody, or anything big, like the law or romance. He is a positivist, able to believe only in what he has proved first-hand for himself. "Now I know," he tells Brigid, after he strip-searched her to see if she has the missing $1,000.

Although he can't believe in any abstract values, he does live by the code of his profession; when that code conflicts with the law, he's on the side of the code.

He accepts the fact that what we conceive of as "reality" is really a series of realities, ever changing. (See Thursby, below.)

Even though he sees the world as chaotic and unpredictable, he feels that man survives not by imitating the seeming chaos of Nature but by imposing his own order in his own area of life.

He obviously believes that logic can overcome crime and even the temptations of irresponsible passions (like his for Brigid).

His basic technique-based on his views of reality and logic-is to stir things up, wait for his antagonists to come to him, and to play them against each other, all the while using a strict positivist logic to find significant relations in the new "realities" his technique uncovers.

Compared with other characters, he is like Brigid a liar and an actor; like Bryan, a believer that the ends justify the means; so like Gutman that this master criminal admiringly invites Spade to join his gang.

Although Spade seems always to be in pursuit of money (even claiming that he fosters a reputation as a crooked sleuth because it brings in well-paying work!), he lives in a modest, even spartan manner. In his tiny apartment, the main room is a living room until he needs to sleep, when it becomes a bedroom. He does not own a car and has to hire a chauffeured vehicle when he needs personal transportation.

When we see in Spade a representative of the hard-hitting American who lives for his job, who trusts nobody, to whom the ends justify the means, a positivist, a pragmatist, a male chauvinist, a loner and a cynic, we must remind ourselves that being like this does not make Spade happy. That is one of Hammett's messages most often overlooked.

Spade's tag-name is Hammett's best. Sam does dig for information like a spade, and, when it serves his purpose, he excels at calling a spade a spade. And it's no accident that Spade has as his given name the (rarely used) first name of Samuel Dashiell Hammett, for eight years a Pinkerton detective.

(For more details about Hammett's characterization of Spade, read the character analyses above of the others with whom he has interacted, and the sections in our "Textual Analysis" titled Characterization: Spade.)

Thursby, Floyd

Another character that we only hear about (from Brigid, Polhaus and Dundy, District Attorney Bryan, Gutman, and Spade), he is important not only to the action but to the development of one of Hammett's main themes: Reality is always a tentative thing, a version that is always ripening for change and revision. In Brigid's first versions, he becomes her ally and lover, whom she ceased to trust and who murdered Archer. According to a presumably more objective account by Polhaus, Thursby was once a bodyguard for a gambler whom he "lost" in the Orient; his troubles seem mainly to have arisen over women who twice have betrayed him to the police. District Attorney Bryan thinks Thursby was killed in a gambler's revenge-vendetta. Gutman's version contradicts Brigid's: Thursby, says "G", was loyal to her and had to be "blipped" by Wilmer as a warning to her to cooperate with "G."

Spade puts all this together to mean that Brigid hired Archer to provoke Thursby, but that didn't work, so she killed Archer to make it look as if Thursby did it.

As always, Hammett distinguishes each character with different physical characteristics: Unlike any of the others, Thursby is athletic and military in his bearing. (See also Characterization: Thursby in our "Textual Analysis" of Hammett's Chapter 1.)

Wise, Sid

Sam's lawyer is wise but very sad in his dealings with his private-eye client. Out of his wisdom, Sid apparently wants Sam to be more trustful and humane, less exploitative. In his sadness, Sid reluctantly yields to Sam's outrageously contradictory demands. On the one hand, Wise is coerced by Sam into pulling strings, using political connections to protect Sam's client Brigid's right to privacy, to confidentiality. On the other hand, Wise is also coerced by Sam-shocked at first but then forced-to violate Iva's right to privacy and confidentiality!

Wise is one of several characters Hammett uses as mirrors to reflect different aspects of Sam's personality. The aspect reflected here is the seedy, desperate, unethical side of Sam.

Hammett distinguishes Wise, in appearance, as the source of a blizzard of dandruff behind a desk piled high with undone work. Sam himself distinguishes Wise as a lawyer who makes so much money protecting Sam in his shady detective work that he should refuse Sam nothing.

THE MALTESE FALCON

THEMES

When we're reading fiction, we're preoccupied-without thinking of it in so many words-with questions like: "What's this all about? What's the author driving at? What's she/he trying to prove?"

THEMES, MOTIFS

In the grip of such questions, we are reflecting on the book's subject, its central ideas, thesis, message, moral, its conclusions and overall meaning. Thinking about our experience on this level, discussing the book with others, dipping into the critics' reactions (as you are now), we find it convenient to use a catchall word: Themes. As we do in music, so with literature: We refer to one aspect of a theme, a sub-theme, as a motif.

THEMES: EXPLICIT

Sometimes an author states his themes explicitly, in his own authorial voice. Thus O. Henry bangs us over the head with the meaning of his story, "The Gift of the Magi." And whole sections of the great muckraker novel *The Jungle* sound as if its author, Upton Sinclair, is writing an editorial or a political speech. And it worked: From President Theodore Roosevelt's administration to President Lyndon Johnson's, pure-food legislation was publicly attributed, in part, to the socialist Sinclair. (See the Monarch Note on *The Jungle*.)

But Dashiell Hammett doesn't state his Falcon themes explicitly in his own voice. He does make some of his message explicit through his characters' beliefs, observations, and conclusions. Thus several of Hammett's themes can be found in statements made by his protagonist, Sam Spade, in dialogue with Brigid O'Shaughnessy, District Attorney Bryan, or Counselor-at-Law Sid Wise. We know that Hammett intends Spade's intellectual observations to be taken as seriously thematic because he makes Sam a sympathetic character (at least, the most sympathetic one). We know Hammett does not intend us to take our philosophy of life from the speeches of Mr. Gutman because Hammett makes him unattractive: His ideas seem to be inherent in his unpleasant personality.

THEMES: IMPLICIT

Hammett also uses the most subtle, most artistic means of thematizing: He allows us to derive his meaning from the conduct and fate of his characters, from the outcome and implications of their action. Thus we learn about Hammett's view of a certain kind of legal personality from District Attorney Bryan's behavior, and the author's attitude toward Brigid's way of life from her fate, which we consider justified. Let us say that Hammett expresses such themes implicitly.

Hammett seems to offer the following ideas, explicit or implicit, as his main themes in *The Maltese Falcon*:

THE PLACE OF ORDER IN HUMAN LIFE

Even though Nature may seem to be controlled by irrational forces, chance, and chaos, the human race can survive only by imposing order, organization, and logic in its own area of reality. This is one of the conclusions we draw from the Parable of Flitcraft, told to Brigid by Spade (Chapter 7). It seems to be a major doctrine of Spade's philosophy, and it can be restated to apply specifically to his work and private life.

LOGIC AND CRIME

Logic can and must prevail over crime and evil in the social sphere, and even over irresponsible passion in the private sphere. While most detective novels work toward the first (social) part of that statement, *The Maltese Falcon* works toward both parts.

GOOD AND EVIL STRIDE TOGETHER

One of the stories within the story in this novel is Gutman's account of the Crusades. And even though it's the villain Gutman who says it, we can consider it as valid because he's merely alluding to a historical fact: " ... the Holy Wars to [the Crusaders] were largely a matter of loot." Even the Book of Genesis of the Hebrew Scriptures makes it (implicitly) clear that good and evil leap-frog each other down through history. Joseph's brothers commit the evil act of selling him into slavery and of telling their father the lie that he was destroyed by a lion. But their evil has good consequences: It puts Joseph in a position in Egypt where he can help them and all of their tribe when the drought hits the Levant. The relevance here is that Sam Spade veers toward evil, and cohorts with evil-doers, in the pursuit of justice. One of the implicit themes of the novel is the mysterious nature of good and evil.

THE NATURE OF GOOD AND EVIL

One aspect of this question is made clear in Falcon, namely, that both good and evil people have many characteristics in common. The master criminal Gutman so admires the methods of the private eye Spade that Gutman invites him to join the "G" - Gang. The criminal Cairo has a certain undeniable charm. Even the totally evil Brigid has the power to raise great sympathy in the highly ethical Effie.

THE ENDS AND THE MEANS

His belief that the ends justify the means has brought Spade success. But also an implicit message in the outcome of the story is that this belief has not brought him happiness. Indeed, it has brought him perilously close to the fate of several criminals who operate on the same basis. It has left him a driven man, with narrow interests, lonely, difficult to get along with, restless and irritable.

U.S.A. CORRUPTION AND VIOLENCE

"Most things in San Francisco can be bought, or taken," Sam tells Brigid, matter-of-factly. We infer that some of her $700 fee has been paid to Wise's contacts to keep her safe from police interrogation. Polhaus also speaks of it as a fact that in St. Louis a gunman is safe from police if he belongs to the Egan mob, and in New York a gunman can stay out of jail if he works for Dixie Monahan. In Hammett's novels *Red Harvest* and *The Glass Key*, whole cities are under the control of gangsters. Although Falcon is set in 1928, when the manufacture and sale of alcoholic liquors is illegal, Spade has no trouble getting rum and even serves it to policemen Polhaus and Dundy. In the other novels, the most respectable Americans sit down with gangsters in speakeasies to enjoy illicit whiskey or gin. In short, a major theme of Hammett's writing is that America is hypocritical in its attitudes toward its own laws, that money and guns buy power, and that Sam Spade's ambiguous ethics could be seen as normal for his time and place. The corruption, violence, and hypocrisy in American life has been a common subject in American fiction, nonfiction, and cinema.

MANIPULATION AND SUCCESS

As Hammett represents it here, success in American life depends on selfish psychological manipulation of other people. In our "Textual Analysis" we shall show how Sam spends whole days in such maneuvers. Steven Marcus, in his classic essay on the Falcon, sees the history of the bird as symbolic of the power struggles and techniques of the capitalist system.

THE ANTAEUS THEME

Spade is emphatic in his belief that a person gains much of her/his strength from being rooted to a specific place on the earth and in a profession. "This is my city and my game," he argues with Gutman. "... you're not in Romeville now," he points out to Wilmer. "You're in my burg." In other words, "You're not where you're strongest; you're where I'm strongest." We may call this Hammett's Antaean theme. Antaeus was a Greek mythic figure who could not be overcome when standing in his own place on the earth. To defeat him, Hercules had to lift him up and hold him high above the ground, to deprive him of the strength he gained by being in touch with Mother Earth.

NEED FOR A CODE

Hammett's private-eye heroes live by a code. His "Continental Op," hero of many Hammett short stories and two novels, works for an agency with such a strict code of ethics that Sam would be ineligible for a job there. But even Sam, with his ambiguous ethics, still observes his own definite code of honor: As he explains to Brigid in the last chapter, he cannot let a criminal go; and he has to catch the killer of a detective even if he didn't like the man, for the reputation of the profession and his place in it. Another part of his code, this motif expressed only in action, is his need to reward those who have helped him (like Polhaus) and to deliver the criminals he publicly pledged (in the D.A.'s office) to deliver. (See the flyting, page 137, as one of Hammett's devices for developing character.)

Notice that even the criminals live by a code. Cairo expected that after Spade disarmed him, Spade would not hit him. Gutman admires Thursby's loyalty to Brigid and regrets her disloyalty to Thursby.

Implicit in much of Hammett's action is the fact that when a Hammett character has to choose between the law and his code, he follows the code. This is a motif of what we have called

Hammett's Antaean theme: A man must be rooted not only in a place but in a "game," a profession.

BEHAVIORISM: A MEANS OF OBSERVING HUMAN CONDUCT

An hypothesis that Hammett at least explores in this novel is the main tenet of the behaviorist school of psychology: That we should not be concerned with studying the inner life- introspection, fantasy, reverie - but with explaining behavior entirely in terms of observable responses to outer stimuli. This psychological method was proposed in Dr. J. B. Watson's writings of 1913 and 1914, and dominated American psychology at the time Hammett wrote *The Maltese Falcon* (and until mid-century). Hammett's method of narration in this 1930 novel is the literary equivalent of the behaviorist method. We know nothing of the inner life of any character except as it manifests itself in her/his external activity. Note the suitability of this approach for "hardboiled fiction." Here we see an instance of method as an implicit theme.

PEIRCEAN THEMES

Hammett himself makes it clear to us that he is indebted to Charles Peirce by rebaptizing Flitcraft as Charles Peirce. Pierce was a major American philosopher whose *Chance, Love, and Logic* appeared posthumously in 1923. The very title of that book, which Hammett at least heard or read about even if he didn't read the work itself, could be considered a subtitle for the Flitcraft parable (Falcon, Chapter 7). There are several other parallels between Peirce's methods and conclusions and Hammett's. Peirce named a third method of reasoning abduction, on the model of the other two methods, induction and deduction. In abduction, the investigator tries to figure out what circumstances could have led to the mystery he is trying to solve. This is a common procedure in detective work. Further, one of Peirce's main themes is that the meaning of an idea is found in its consequences. This is true of Spade's work; for example, his amoral methods, he thinks, must be judged by his results. Further, Peirce revised his philosophical system every time (four in all) that he made a new discovery in logic. This is clearly how a detective operates too: For him what appears to be the true explanation must be subjected to continual revision as new factors are discovered. Two extreme examples of reality under revision occur in Sam's interrogations of Brigid, who gives several different versions of what's going on, and in the questioning by the police of Brigid, Cairo, and Sam in Chapter 8, when an absurd explanation of events becomes the one adopted, by necessity. More typical of the revision process is the fact that at one point it seems sure that Thursby killed Archer, even though Spade has known from the beginning who the real killer is.

THE MALTESE FALCON

PLOT STRUCTURE, TECHNIQUES, AND STYLE

OTHER FACTORS IN HAMMETT'S SUCCESS

As we have seen, (1) Hammett's boldness in addressing some of the major themes of our century is surely one factor in his fame as a novelist. Other factors also important are: (2) his masterful control of plot, that is, the way he excites our curiosity and then deeply satisfies it, the way he structures his content; (3) his creation of about 20 memorable characters whose dialogue is famous for its American sound and its inclusion of American slang of the Twenties; (4) his skillful blend of the techniques of traditional detective fiction, Zolaism, mainstream fiction, and his own brand of "hardboiled fiction"; (5) his original use of language that is so compact, so economical it is often compared with Ernest Hemingway's, although it is distinctly Hammett's in its tone. These characteristics in combination raise *The Maltese Falcon* far above its genre (detective fiction) to the level of "art fiction."

PLOT VS. STORY

Our first step in appreciating Hammett's design of his plot is to distinguish between plot and story. An author must first have in mind a story, that is, an account that follows the chronological order in which his events actually occur. Then he must fashion a plot which follows a scrambled, nonchronological order in which he decides to reveal these events. In the finished fiction, of course plot becomes the order in which the characters concurrently (1) discover past events and (2) live their present lives. Let's now see how Hammett has converted raw story into artistic plot.

RAW STORY: THREE STRANDS

In his introduction to his 1934 edition of Falcon Hammett tells us that he combined three strands into his narrative. First was historical information that intrigued him about "the peculiar rental agreement between Charles V and the Order of the Hospital of Saint John of Jerusalem." The second element was a situation he had explored in his story "The Gutting of Couffignal." The hero is supposedly torn between his duty as a detective to arrest a certain female criminal, and the temptation to accept her offer of sex if he lets her go free. The third element was the final setting he had used in his story. "The Whosis Kid." It's a small apartment in which the crisis and climax are intensified because the five criminals and one detective are crowded into a confining space. Hammett felt he had not done justice to either of the last two situations and thought he'd have "better luck with these two failures" if he "combined them with the Maltese lease in a longer story."

RAW STORY: HISTORICAL BACKGROUND

Adding characters and situations needed to develop his three strands of narrative, Hammett now worked out a story that is mainly historical in its sixteenth-century beginnings and increasingly fictitious thereafter.

In 1530 the Holy Roman Emperor, Charles V, gave the Knights of St. John lands including the island of Malta. The only tribute he required of them was "presentation of a yearly falcon on All-Saints Day." So grateful were they, they sent him not an ordinary live falcon but a golden facsimile, a statuette encrusted with jewels. But this "Maltese falcon" was stolen by pirates and for almost 400 years passed from one owner to another, in Algeria, Italy, France, and finally Turkey. In 1928, Hammett decided, it was in the possession of a Russian General Kemidov.

RAW STORY: PLOT DEVELOPMENT

Conflict is the essence of fiction (and drama). Hammett introduces conflict and necessary tensions by creating a certain Mr. Gutman who had been searching for the bird since about 1911 and had located it late in 1928. He tried to buy it from Kemidov in Constantinople. That failing, Gutman sent his "agent," a seductive woman, to steal it.

This seductive woman is Hammett's femme fatale, a literary type, a beautiful woman who uses her sexual charm to lure men into dangers and even disaster. Hammett triggers the conflicts in his story by having the femme fatale, Brigid, steal the falcon not for Gutman but for herself. First she gets a Levantine, Joel Cairo, to help her. After they steal the bird, she asks gunman Floyd Thursby, to help her "ditch" Cairo and get the falcon to California. Once in California, Brigid hatches a plan to get rid of Thursby. She hires a private detective, Miles Archer, in hopes that either the detective will kill Thursby, or Thursby will kill the detective and be sent to jail, leaving Brigid alone in possession of the fabulously valuable statuette.

Brigid's plans are unsuccessful and she kills Archer with Thursby's gun. Archer's partner, Sam Spade, arrives on the scene of the killing, reenacts the shooting with police-detective Polhaus, and then quickly leaves. Alone in his apartment, he quickly deduces that Brigid killed Archer and decides he will not expose her to the police until she leads him, unwittingly or not, to the other criminals.

PLOT: IN MEDIAS RES

Notice that Hammett's first requirement, in converting his raw story into a plot, was to decide where to start. In 1530? Don't laugh. That's where John Huston started his film version: With a little summary of the falcon's history rolling upward on a drum. In 1911, when Gutman starts his search for the falcon? That would postpone the appearance of Sam and Brigid, the main characters. Artistic novelists, like Hammett, start in medias res (Latin for "in the middle of things"), rolling the action forward and "backward) at the same time. So Hammett starts in late 1928, with Rigid's appearance in Sam's office to hire the detective she needs for her scheme to eliminate Thursby.

PLOT: FLASHBACKS

Ever since Homer, good story-tellers have used a simple device to reveal past action. In the midst of the present, ongoing action, the author contrives to reveal past events in flashbacks. Thus Gutman tells Sam the story of the falcon as late as Chapter 13! By then the recitation of the story is fully motivated, our curiosity ripe for it. Similarly, in Chapter 19, Gutman is forced to tell Spade about Brigid's past, and in Chapter 20, Brigid is forced to reveal the details of her killing of Archer.

Thus Homer told the story of *The Odyssey* - the action of which takes twenty years - all in the last 17 days! And Hammett tells the story of *The Maltese Falcon* - the action of which occurs over 398 years -all in the last five days!

PLOT: POSTPONED REVELATIONS

Comparing the raw story with the finished plot, we see that Hammett created greater suspense by withholding as much information as he possibly could for as long as he could. In the chronological account, e.g., we learn that Spade deduced who killed Archer just hours after she did it. By letting Sam keep those thoughts to himself (we'll talk about Point of View soon), Hammett lets us think that maybe Brigid and Polhaus are both right: Thursby did kill Archer. Thus Hammett keeps us in suspense on the matter for 18 chapters! And since Hammett begins his plot well after Brigid and Cairo stole the falcon, we don't know even that they do know each other until Spade surprises Brigid by telling her he knows. One more example: We learn in Chapter 10 that Spade found in Brigid's apartment a "week-old receipt for the ... rent." Sam keeps the meaning of that discovery secret for another ten chapters.

OVERALL CHAPTER ORGANIZATION

Looking back, we can see that Hammett has organized his plot in three segments. (1) It takes Spade the first eleven chapters to complete his plan of locating all the criminals involved. (2) Then, from Chapters 12 to 17, his situations all become more complicated until, at the end of 17, it seems he is going down to defeat. (3) But in the final three chapters, by playing the criminals against each other and contriving to have Brigid alone at the end, he puts all the pieces together, solves three murders, resolves his affair with the femme fatale, sends four criminals to their just deserts, and saves himself from serious trouble with the police and the district attorney.

INDIVIDUAL CHAPTER ORGANIZATION

In addition to using his 20 chapters to build the three-part overall structure, Hammett designs a dramatic form for every separate chapter. For example: Chapter 1, which brings the two main characters together and launches the action, is framed by Brigid's arrival and departure. Chapter 11 is framed by Wilmer's arrival at Gutman's in a state of humiliation and his departure in a state of triumph. Chapter 14 -a busy chapter with four scenes and eight settings - is framed by Effie, with whom Spade confers at the beginning and the end. Chapters 6, 15, and 16 are structured according to an ebb-and-flow pattern. Six and 16 both alternate between quiet sequences and more sensational ones. In 15, the first scene lessens the pressures on Sam, the second increases them.

HAMMETT'S POINT OF VIEW

Much of Hammett's success in postponing revelations, creating suspense, and representing life as "hardboiled" is due to the point of view he uses. By point of view we mean that point in human awareness from which the action is observed and related. Usually an author has several options:

FIRST PERSON NARRATOR

He or she can turn the job of narrator over to a character who tells the story in the first person: I, we, ours, mine. This has the advantage that we can identify with one person, knowing that person's thoughts, private reactions, doubts, suspicions, conclusions. It has the disadvantage that we can know only what the narrator knows. But suppose he is curious to know more? That's the case with Emily Bronte's narrator in Wuthering Heights: he's a minor character far from the center of the action but eager to learn as much as he can.

The reader can get even closer to the action if the narrator is a major character. Thus Jules Verne has Professor Arronax tell the story of Captain Nemo in *Twenty Thousand Leagues Under the Sea*. And the gap between the reader and the central action can be closed entirely if the author lets the hero/ine tell his/her own story. That's what Dashiell Hammett does in many short stories and two novels, *Red Harvest* and *The Dain Curse*, in which the hero-narrator is the anonymous "Continental

Op." Suspense is lessened, though, because we know that if he is telling us the story then he survived the terrors of the situation.

THIRD-PERSON NARRATOR

Or an author can switch the point of view and tell the story him/herself, in the third person: She, he, they, hers. He can become the author omniscient, with the godlike power to stand over his creation and give us an overall view or to zoom in for a closeup. He can show us a character as she appears to others, from the outside, and then he can put us inside her mind, inside the minds of any or all of his characters. He can take us back and forth across time and show us how separated, seemingly unrelated events are really solidly connected. Examples of novels related by the author omniscient are Nathaniel Hawthorne's *The House of The Seven Gables* and Kurt Vonnegut's *Breakfast of Champions*.

AUTHOR AS LIMITED NARRATOR.

Or an author can still tell the story her/himself but focus mainly on one character. He limits himself to what that one character can do, think, feel. The reader gets the benefit of identifying with one person and also of greater suspense: If that character is not telling the story, we don't know whether she/he survives. An example of an author limiting himself to the point of view of a minor character is Joseph Conrad's "The Lagoon;" to that of a major character, Chuck Wachtel's *Joe the Engineer*.

AUTHOR AS OBJECTIVE NARRATOR

So far we have considered points of view from which the author can take us inside a character's mind, making us privy to that character's opinions, sensations, secret ambitions. The author has still another option, while still telling his story in the third person. He can stay outside all characters. A famous example is Hemingway's "The Killers." We identify with no one person. We observe everybody and everything "objectively," as a camera and a tape recorder would report on life.

HAMMETT'S COMBINATION

Which option does Hammett use? He does tell the story in the third person. And he focuses on one character: Sam Spade. There is never any action if Spade isn't there. But we are never inside Spade! So what Hammett has done is combine two points of view-that of the author limited to one person, and that of the author as objective narrator.

Thus the reader is never privy to Spade's feelings or his thought processes, unless he reveals them in speech or action. This greatly increases the suspense. When Spade sits on his bed thinking about the murder of Archer, we do not know that he has concluded that Brigid is the killer. When he picks up the week-old rent receipt, we don't know what it means to him. Twice, when alone, he mutters something aloud. It makes no sense to us because we don't know what he was thinking before and after. In *The Maltese Falcon* Hammett hit on the point-of-view most calculated to heighten the mystery.

BEHAVIORIST POINT OF VIEW

What shall we call Hammett's new combination? If we were to name those we discussed first, they would be: character as narrator (first person); author as omniscient narrator, or as limited narrator, or as objective narrator (third person). We think we have the right name for Hammett's blending of the limited and the objective narrators. It seems that starting in 1913, just 15 years before Hammett wrote Falcon, a psychologist named John Watson proposed a new approach to human behavior: Ignore the inner processes-reverie, memory, dreams, fantasy, logic - and study the meaning of a person's behavior from its outward manifestations. The new science, popular for most of Hammett's life, was called behaviorism. Let's call Hammett's new approach the behaviorist point of view.

TECHNIQUES OF CHARACTERIZATION

Hammett uses eight methods for individualizing the people in Falcon. (1) The first is the Watson technique, applied now to detective fiction. (2) Hammett's simplest technique is his use of tag-names. He tags many of his characters with a name that emphasizes one aspect of a personality. A detective who digs for facts is named Spade; another who is both the hunter and the hunted is named Archer (after the constellation Sagittarius). (3) One of Hammett's strongest techniques is his colorful physical description of each character when she/he makes her/his first appearance. There are three such descriptions in the first two pages! Hammett follows through with detailed descriptions of a character's movements and facial expressions as he interacts with others. Thus when we first get a glimpse of Spade's naked body, it's like a bear's; when he gets ready to knock a man out, a dreamlike expression comes over his face. (4) Hammett will also characterize a person by the way another character sees him. At first we know Thursby only from Brigid's description of him. Later we get Gutman's view of Thursby. In other words, by the way Character A describes Character B, Character A is also, to some extent, describing himself. (5) Hammett prefers to show rather than tell, so his favorite method of revealing character is self-characterization: Each character reveals his/her own nature through his/her action. By his interrupting other people, Spade reveals his impatience and his disregard for their feelings. By his thinking of something another detective overlooks, Spade shows he is more methodical, more thorough.

DIALOGUE CHARACTERIZES.

(6) Hammett gives each person his/her characteristic way of talking. Iva Archer gushes; Brigid stumbles over the emotions she is acting out. Cairo strives for pithy, well-rounded sentences; Gutman is loquacious. (7) Hammett also enhances his characters by (implicitly) comparing and contrasting them. Thus he contrasts two police detectives mainly in the way they relate to Spade: Dundy is eager to find fault with Spade, Polhaus is more tolerant, trying to weigh the best in Spade against his bad characteristics. (8) Hammett also uses an epic literary technique not often found in contemporary literature: the flyting. This is a contest in verbal abuse which usually ends with each contestant boasting about what he can and will do. The boaster is expected to live up to his boast and knows he'd better. Hammett's greatest flyting is Spade's farewell speech to the district attorney that closes Chapter 15.

(For detailed analyses of characterization, see "Twenty Character Studies in *The Maltese Falcon*.")

Hammett's themes and situations give him plenty of opportunity to demonstrate his talent for irony. That's the name we give to devices authors use to explore the differences between appearance and reality.

We say a writer is using verbal irony when she/he, or a character, says one thing but means another, or when a character says more than she realizes, or says something apparently true but soon to be proved false.

As a cynical, "hardboiled" person, Spade uses irony to cut his way through one situation after another. When he chides Archer with: "You've got brains, yes you have," we know he means exactly the opposite. Love and affection especially provoke irony from him: "The course of true love," he says pointing to Wilmer's annoyance at Cairo's caresses, and he makes it a point to refer to Brigid as "angel" or "my own true love." But sometimes Spade's irony is not deliberate. He proposes a toast to Dundy and Polhaus: "Success to crime." He probably means "Since we make our living fighting it, here's to more of it." But to Dundy at least it must sound suspicious: The lieutenant, we soon discover, suspects Spade of just having committed homicide.

Gutman comes off badly in an ironic interchange of ideas about ownership in Chapter 13, and again, at the end when he says, "We're none of us dead yet," just minutes before Wilmer guns him down.

We say an author is using dramatic irony when he creates situations in which a character acts in ignorance of the facts, facts known to other characters and to the reader. For example, in Chapter 2 Spade asks Polhaus whether Thursby lived alone at his hotel. When Polhaus answers "Alone," he can't know what that means to Spade and to us: There was no sister Corinne.

Again, at the end of Chapter 8, Dundy suspects that the reason Spade won't let the police enter his apartment is that Mrs. Archer is inside. The reader knows that there's a worse situation inside than mere proof that Spade and Iva are lovers. Then Cairo yells, "Help! Police!": deliciously ironic, coming from a criminal.

The Maltese Falcon resonates with irony. All these people are risking death for a "gold" statuette that proves to be a fake. Brigid thinks she has Sam on a string because he has enjoyed her sexual favors, while actually he's giving her a few days' freedom to help him round up all the criminals. And as Sam makes clear repeatedly, you can't be sure that anybody is what he/she says he/she is.

HAMMETT AND ZOLA

Emile Zola, the French novelist and literary theoretician, advocated (1880) a new fiction based on Darwinism. The novelist, he said (and he practiced this himself), must meticulously report all the facts about his characters' hereditary and environmental influences, and about the techniques they use to survive. He must be sure to see to it that the action and the outcome are true resultants of those situations. Zola especially hated the "plot" that is manipulated to provide a "happy ending."

Hammett is obviously not a 100 percent Zolaist. We know next to nothing about the early background of his characters. But Hammett is a Zolaist in at least three ways: (1) He gives us precise details about how a detective searches a house, disarms an opponent, works with others in his trade, and even how he rolls a cigarette. (2) Hammett is also faithful to Zola's demand for a true ending. Spade works scientifically and produces scientific results. But his five days of hard and dangerous work have not made him happy in any other area of his life. He is practically back where he started so far as human relations are concerned, no richer in any sense except in work experience, and he is perhaps more cynical now. (3) Finally, Hammett is also Zolaist in his attention to the present (but not the past) environment in which his characters work and live: that is, the setting of the action.

SETTING

Hammett is a Zolaist in his fidelity to real environments but not a believer in Zola's use of massive detail. And as a writer of "hardboiled fiction," especially, Hammett honestly admits America has seedy locales as well as pretty places. He feels most comfortable, apparently, in describing places he knows well, perhaps because he can test the accuracy of his words against what's really there: his own apartment on Post Street, the restaurant where he has eaten pig's feet. He uses the classical Homeric method of describing a setting: He lets us discover a corner of an apartment or of a city only when the focal character moves in that direction.

And so we know only the bedroom of Spade's apartment the first time we're in it. We see his "tinny alarm clock" only when he looks at it. Later, we explore his kitchen, and later yet, the bathroom. We move with him to the "grating and rattling" elevator door, through "yellow-walled corridors" and a dark narrow court, we stand near "bare ugly stairs."

These places are made plainer yet by contrast (always one of Hammett's favorite devices) as Spade walks through a "long purplish lobby" on his way to one hotel suite with a mahogany door and plush chairs, or to another with a "red and cream sitting room" with flowers in "pottery vases of black and silver." Setting here serves the function of letting us see how well the criminals (and other well-off people) live as compared with working people like Sam and Effie.

The importance of setting to Hammett is also made clear by his deliberately experimenting with "apartment drama." Several times in Falcon he brings together several characters-criminals, police, or both-in the compressed space of Sam's "rooms." On one occasion, the apartment seems small enough to be a cozy haven for lovers. On others, it's a place too small to contain the fury. The entire story converges on that place.

METAPHOR: SIMILE

A metaphor is a figure of speech that declares a similarity between dissimilar things. Metaphor helps a writer explain the unknown in terms of the known. And the surprise a writer sparks in his reader with such unexpected comparisons helps the writer control the reader's emotional reactions.

Hammett uses poetic devices so sparingly that they have thereby a greater effect. He focuses attention on Gutman's "great soft egg of a belly." Spade wants to know if Effie sees Brigid as "a madonna." He describes Iva's activities as "merry-go-round riding."

Hammett's at his best with the special type of metaphor called simile: The comparison is established with a "like" or "as." Thus Gutman has "a hand like a fat pink star." And Flitcraft disappeared "like a fist when you open your hand."

SYMBOLISM

A symbol is a person, place, or thing that stands for something else, something larger than itself, maybe a material thing that suggests something immaterial. A symbol is not experienced all at once, like a simile, but rather grows on us. Thus the Maltese falcon becomes a symbol for greed and vanity. Spade is often seen as symbolizing the pragmatic, success-driven, American workaholic. Symbols can help an author create an emotional state because we experience them subliminally. Hammett describes Spade as slicing a long slender loaf of bread, and mashing a cigarette in a dish, while Brigid caresses the "body and barrel" of a pistol, all Freudian phallic images used just before the two make love.

LITERARY AND CULTURAL ALLUSIONS

Hammett was consciously writing serious literature (as opposed to genre literature) and so did not hesitate to use allusions to other authors, thinkers, composers. In Falcon you will find allusions to the philosopher Charles Peirce, the poets Vergil and Shakespeare, the historian H. G. Wells, and the composers Bach and Wilhelmj. These allusions are discussed in our "Textual Analysis."

STYLE

His irony, metaphor, symbolism, and choice details account for some of the quality of Hammett's prose. But his diction and his syntax account for most of it. Three out of every four of Hammett's words are monosyllables. That usually includes the key words: In one scene the key words are fist, beam, lid, lift, frisked, life. One out of every five of Hammett's words is an action verb: in one paragraph, e.g., walk, kicked, held, stumbled, hear, watch. Ninety-eight out of a hundred Hammett words are of Anglo-Saxon derivation (as opposed to words of Latin or French origin). His dialogue is "hard-boiled" because it's laconic, urgent, and (with most characters) to the point; it's replete with blasphemous curses (omitted in some editions) like "for Christ's sake!," "O Jesus," "I hope to Christ" and slang: In our "Textual Analysis" we will define about 75 slang expressions Hammett uses.

Hammett's sentences are usually short (averaging 13 words), and when they're long, it's for a special effect. The syntax is simple. Notice, e.g., the parallelism in these two sentences:

They walked across and across the floor, the girl falteringly, with incoordinate steps, Sam surely, on the balls of his feet with balance unaffected by her staggering. Her face was chalk-white and eyeless, his sullen, with eyes hardened to watch everywhere at once.

To appreciate the compactness and pithiness of Hammett's prose, try to paraphrase a passage. You might well need more words than he used. William Marling, author of an excellent handbook on Hammett, characterizes Hammett's economical prose as using, "in few words, devices of tone, transition, and plot long thought to require more space."

(For more details on any topic discussed in this chapter, check for that topic in our "Textual Analysis.")

THE MALTESE FALCON

IDEAS FOR PAPERS, ORAL REPORTS, AND CLASS DISCUSSION

....

Majoring in psychology? To what extent can you see John B. Watson's and Sigmund Freud's influences on TMF? Start with our numerous references to these two psychologists, then peruse Watson's Behavior: An Introduction to Comparative Psychology (1914) and Freud's General Introductory Lectures to Psychoanalysis (1919).

Hammett told friends that TMF was written partly under the influence of Henry James's Wings of the Dove. Note that in each work a romantic affair cannot survive the evil the lovers have perpetrated. See any other parallels in plot/characterization? To what extent was Hammett being facetious? E.g., the ship that carries the falcon is called La Paloma (the dove) and James uses Dove in his title and in his symbolism . . .

Read all five of Hammett's novels and report on the progress of love in Hammett's characterizations. Or limit your topic to a comparison of the nature of love in TMF (Sam and Brigid) and in *The Thin Man* (Nick and Nora).

Report on the extent to which Spade's code is based on the doctrines laid down by Hammett's boss at Pinkerton.

Compare the "Continental Op's" code with Spade's and/or James Wright's.

Explain the unusual point of view Hammett has adopted for this novel. (Review all the passages labeled Point of View.) What advantages has Hammett reaped by combining the two points of view of author as limited narrator and author as objective narrator? How does the result approximate the effects produced by drama on stage or on film/tape? Why have we here called it behaviorist?

Read one or more of the "Continental Op" stories, written in the first-person point of view. Contrast the effects Hammett achieves in the "Op" mode with those in the Falcon (third person objective) mode.

Partly as Gutman's way of justifying his own evil, partly as Hammett's way of developing a theme, Gutman stresses the fact that the Crusades were as much a matter of looting as of defense of Christianity. Do some research on this aspect of the Crusades, and relate it to TMF.

Compare Hammett's use of the Crusades as literary material with Kurt Vonnegut's in Slaughterhouse-Five (which is subtitled: The Children's Crusade, after one of the most evil of the Crusades).

Report on the actual places in San Francisco that Hammett models his settings on. For a more thorough report, read the North Point Press edition of TMF.

Some American authors became all-out Zolaists (Theodore Dreiser, Frank Norris, the early Norman Mailer, e.g.). Others used some Zolaist techniques and ignored others. Review our paragraphs on "Zolaism." To what extent was Hammett a Zolaist?

Report on Hammett's use of tag-names: Spade, Flitcraft, Pierce, Le Blanc, Brigid, Perine, et al. What effect do tag-names have, what functions do they perform?

Read Three Women in our "Textual Analysis" of Hammett's Chapter 3. Check the handbooks of mythology. Use Marling as a takeoff or peg if you need additional academic authentication. Why does Hammett use this mythic background?

Read three or four biographies of Hammett (starting with the earliest) plus encyclopedia articles about him. How many "myths" about him have been corrected by the later biographers (Marling and Layman, to start with)? Why do authors create a mythic background for themselves?

Review here our remarks on the Prohibition Era. Read Steven Marcus' classic essay on Hammett. How does TMF show that Americans of the Twenties engaged in mass hypocrisy? Why was Repeal necessary?

[Is there any parallel to the "war against drugs?" This bracketed question should be cleared with your instructor first: Extending your scope this much might be considered too much or too tangential.]

Show how Hammett's descriptions of the changes in facial expressions of characters in verbal or physical combat bear out the Watson-behaviorist approach to the study of character.

Report on street and/or underworld and/or outcast slang as they figure in TMF. An intensive study of five terms would suffice for a short paper; fifteen properly handled might suffice for a term paper. Some 75 such locutions are covered in the Note. Move from there to the dictionaries of slang, Webster's Third International, the William and Mary Morris Dictionaries, etc.

In Diane Johnson's brilliant study of Hammett she sees the private eye and the criminal as two parts of the same personality (the superego and the id, respectively). That's how she explains their "affinity," as we called it in our "Textual Analysis" of Hammett's Chapter 5. Report on the Johnson view as applied to Spade and Gutman/Cairo/Brigid.

Relate Diane Johnson's superego-id idea to James Wright's advice to Hammett. Show how the James Wright advice (our page 2) gives the private eye inordinate power. Use Hammett's short story "The Golden Horseshoe" and/or the ways Spade takes the law into his own hands.

Read William Marling's discussion of how Walker Gibson's analysis of "tough style" applies to Hammett. For a more intensive study, read Gibson's *Tough, Sweet, and Stuffy*.

Compare a novel by Raymond Chandler (*The Big Sleep*?) with TMF. Use the analysis of techniques in our "Plot Structure, Techniques, and Style" as your model for analyzing Chandler's.

Report on Raymond Chandler's estimate of Hammett in his *The Simple Art of Murder*. What has Chandler added to your study of Hammett that was not covered in class or in this Note?

BIBLIOGRAPHY

Writings By Dashiell Hammett

Hammett, Dashiell. *Red Harvest*. New York: Random House, 1929. New York: Vintage, 1972.

Hammett, Dashiell. *The Dain Curse*. New York: Random House, 1929. New York: Vintage, 1972.

Hammett, Dashiell. *The Maltese Falcon*. New York: Random House, 1930. New York: Vintage, 1972.

Hammett, Dashiell. *The Glass Key*. New York: Random House, 1931. New York: Vintage, 1972.

Hammett, Dashiell. *The Thin Man*. New York: Random House, 1934. New York: Vintage, 1972.

Hammett, Dashiell. *The Maltese Falcon*. With a new introduction by the author. New York: Modern library, 1934.

Valuable information on the way he conceived of the book and on models for his characters.

Hammett, Dashiell, and Robert Colodny. *The Battle of the Aleutians*. Adak, Alaska: Intelligence Section, Field Force Headquarters, Adak, 1944.

Hammett, Dashiell. *Dead Yellow Women*. Edited by Ellery Queen. New York: Spivak, 1946.

A collection of six Hammett stories, some of them not available elsewhere.

Hammett, Dashiell. *The Dashiell Hammett Story Omnibus*. Edited and with an introduction by Lillian Hellman. London: Cassell, 1960.

Hammett, Dashiell. *The Big Knockover: Selected Stories and Short Novels*. Edited and with an Introduction by Lillian Hellman. New York: Random House, 1966.

The introduction is a major memoir; her selection of stories includes Tulip, the autobiographical novel that Hammett never finished. The main character, "Pop," reminisces about his time in jail, in the army, and meditates on the ways to tell a story. Totally different style from that of the "hardboiled" fiction.

Hammett, Dashiell. *Novels*. New York: Knopf, 1966.

Hammett, Dashiell. *The Maltese Falcon*. San Francisco: North Point Press, 1987.

Illustrated with photographs of the places mentioned in the text, with annotations by Glenn Todd.

Hammett, Dashiell. *The Continental Op*. With an introduction by Steven Marcus. New York: Random House, 1974. New York: Vintage, 1975.

The best stories about the "Op" together with one of the best essays on Hammett.

Writings About Dashiell Hammett

Bazelon, David T. "Dashiell Hammett's 'Private Eye.' No Loyalty beyond the Job." Commentary, May 1949.

Chandler, Raymond. *The Simple Art of Murder*. New York: Ballantine, 1972.

A major study of American detective fiction, including brilliant insights into the work of Hammett by the only contemporary writer qualified to stand beside him.

Giannetti, Louis. *Masters of American Cinema*. Englewood Cliffs, N.J.: Prentice-Hall, 1981.

Good starting place for research on John Huston's film version of *The Maltese Falcon*.

Gibson, Walker. *Tough, Sweet, and Stuffy*. Bloomington: Indiana University Press, 1975.

His analysis of "tough" style is helpful in understanding Hammett's effects. Use it in conjunction with Marling (below).

Hellman, Lillian. *An Unfinished Woman: A Memoir*. Boston: Little, Brown, 1969. Many valuable anecdotes about Hammett plus her essay on him which is also her Introduction to *The Big Knockover* (see Hammett above).

Hellman, Lillian. *Pentimento: A Book of Portraits*. Boston: Little, Brown, 1973.

Many valuable anecdotes about Hammett.

Hellman, Lillian. *Scoundrel Time*. Boston: Little, Brown, 1976.

Hellman's experiences and impressions of the McCarthy era, including an account of her and Hammett's troubles during the "witch-hunts."

Hellman, Lillian. *Three*. Boston: Little, Brown, 1979.

One-volume edition of her three books of memoirs.

Howe, Irving, and Lewis Coser. *The American Communist Party*. New York: Praeger, 1962.

A Study of CP policies and tactics during the period when Hammett was alleged to have been a member.

Johnson, Diane. *Dashiell Hammett: A Life*. New York: Random House, 1983.

A well-researched biography that also attempts to catch the moods and attitudes of its subject. Johnson is herself a novelist.

Klein, Carole. "Red Brick and Brownstone: A Literary Tour of Gramercy Park." New York Times Book Review, March 13, 1988.

About Hammett and others who lived in or passed through this New York neighborhood.

Layman, Richard. *Dashiell Hammett: A Descriptive Bibliography*. Pittsburgh, Pennsylvania: University of Pittsburgh Press, 1979.

Essential to all serious research on Hammett.

Layman, Richard. *Shadow Man: The Life of Dashiell Hammett*. New York: Harcourt Brace Jovanovich, 1981. This extraordinary piece of research set the record straight on many matters in the life and times of Hammett.

Macdonald, Ross. *On Crime Writing.* Santa Barbara, California: Capra, 1973. Himself a writer of crime fiction, Macdonald has many insightful things to say about *The Maltese Falcon.*

Marcus, Steven. "Dashiell Hammett and the Continental Op." Partisan Review, 41 (1975) 363. Probably the most valuable single essay on Hammett. Also appears as part of his introduction to *The Continental Op* (see Hammett, above), and in the Most and Stowe anthology (see below).

Marling, William. *Dashiell Hammett.* Boston: Twayne, 1983.

For the student, this is the best introduction to the life and works of Hammett.

Most, Glenn W., and William W. Stowe, editors. *The Poetics of Murder: Detective Fiction and Literary Theory.* New York: Harcourt Brace Jovanovich, 1983.

Contains Steven Marcus' essay on Hammett as well as other classic essays on the genre.

Mundell, E. H. *A List of the Original Appearances of Dashiell Hammett's Magazine Work.* Kent State, Ohio: Kent State University Press, 1968.

Navasky, Victor. *Naming Names.* New York: Viking, 1980.

Hammett knew that giving the names of contributors to the bail fund would subject them to harassment, loss of jobs, blacklisting, etc. Navasky studies the moral predicament of many persons caught in this crossfire during the days of the "witch-hunts" and the McCarthy Era.

Nolan, *William F. Dashiell Hammett: A Casebook.* With an introduction by Philip Durham. Santa Barbara, California: McNally & Loftin, 1969.

The first, and still the most uncritically admiring, study of Hammett, since updated by Nolan's own 1983 book, but still good reading.

Nolan, *William F. Hammett: A Life at the Edge*. New York: Congdon & Weed/St. Martin's, 1983.

Valuable impressions of a lifelong student of Hammett.

Peirce, Charles Sanders. *Chance, Love, and Logic*. New York: Harcourt, Brace, and Co., 1923.

Hammett certainly read this book or heard about it enough to call one of his characters -concerned with chance and logic - "Charles Pierce" (a.k.a. Flitcraft).

Shaw, Joseph T., editor. *The Hard-Boiled Omnibus: Early Stories from Black Mask.*

Shaw encouraged Hammett during some of his most difficult days. Not only early Hammett is here but also Carroll John Daly, who pioneered "hard-boiled" fiction.

Skenazy, Paul. *The New Wild West: The Urban Mysteries of Dashiell Hammett and Raymond Chandler.* Boise, Idaho: Boise State University, 1982.

Skenazy picked up an idea from Chapter 18 of *The Maltese Falcon* and has done well by both authors.

Symons, Julian. *Bloody Murder: From the Detective Story to the Crime Novel: A History.* New York: Viking, 1984.

A completely revised edition of his 1972 book, *The Mortal Consequences: A History from ...*

Watson, John Broadus. *Behavior: An Introduction to Comparative Psychology.* New York: Henry Holt, 1914.

Hammett's point of view in TMF is the literary equivalent of Watson's approach to behavior.

Wolfe, Peter. *Beams Falling: The Art of Dashiell Hammett*. Bowling Green, Ohio: Bowling Green University Press, 1980.

New facts, new insights: provocative.